2/23/16

Mark –
My new cooking and literary
friend at DRC.

I hope you enjoy these _true_
stories.
Mark

An Unconventional Childhood

Growing Up in the Catskill Mountains During the 1950s and 1960s

An Unconventional Childhood

Growing Up in the Catskill
Mountains
During the 1950s and 1960s

By
Marilyn Mayes Kaltenborn

To order additional copies of this title, contact your favorite local bookstore or visit www.tbmbooks.com Cover design by The Troy Book Makers, Book design by Marilyn Mayes Kaltenborn. Revised edition. Printed in the United States of America The Troy Book Makers www.thetroybookmakers.com ISBN: 978-1-61468-158-8

To my parents
Murray and Bertha Mayes

For Their Grandchildren
Nell, Zachary, and Hal

Contents

Forward and Acknowledgments

After I retired, I took an adult education writing class at my local high school. As part of that class and as part of a writers' group, I wrote a few stories about growing up in the small Catskill Mountain village of Fleischmanns, New York, in the 1950s and 1960s. People liked my stories. I then realized I had a lot of true stories about the unconventional things my brothers and I were allowed to do as children. So, I decided to write about them. This book is the result.

One of the remarkable things that happened while I was writing the stories is that I located my very best childhood friend, Dick Pultz. It was through the miracle of the Internet. We sent e-mails to each other, and then my husband and I visited Dick and his wife for a few days two years ago. It was wonderful. In so many ways, he is the same old Dick that I remember.

Of course, as time passes, our memories of events fade. Or, in some cases, they may never have been exactly accurate. Where my memory was weak, my brothers, Brian and Dean, helped me. They read my stories and suggested corrections, which I nearly always accepted. Dick, too, was very helpful. As children, my cousin Danny and I played together all the time, and he appears in many of my stories. He says he remembers almost nothing of his childhood. As a result, he hasn't disputed the accuracy of what I have written. But, at the end of the day, I accept responsibility for all of the inaccuracies in the book.

The information that accompanies the photos is, to the best of my memory, accurate. In many cases, the dates accompanying my stories and the photos are my estimate. My father took most of the photos that are in the book, unless, of course, he is in the photo. He had a timer that allowed him to be in a photo, but I don't remember him using the device very often. I do remember when he bought a handheld light meter. It was the latest invention and he loved using it. He had a single-lens reflex camera and used Kodachrome or, in later years, Ektachrome film. He took his film in the canister it came in to Muller's Store on Main Street to be sent away to Kodak to be developed. Most of the film was developed into slides. Every time he got his slides back, he set up the slide projector and the screen in the dining room and the whole family sat around viewing the photos.

Many of the slides I found were of roses. I know it was difficult to grow tea roses in Fleischmanns, and I remember how happy my parents were when the roses survived the winter and produced flowers. But seriously, how many times did Dad need to photo them?

My husband, H. Stanley Kaltenborn, Jr., and I scanned the slides and paper photos, except we threw out most of the slides of those damn roses.

Oh, I must also thank Stan for encouraging me to write this book and for reading it more than once.

Chapter 1

My First Memory

Brian and me in the living room, 1957

In June 1952, I was nearly three. More than once that June, I stood by the cherry drop-leaf table that had been in my mother's family for generations. It was one of many of Mother's prized family possessions.

My mother, Bertha Cowan Mayes, grew up on the Cowan family dairy farm just outside the tiny Catskill Mountain village of New Kingston, New York.

New Kingston is about a thirty-minute drive from
Fleischmanns, where I lived. Grandma Cowan lived in
her house in the village of New Kingston during the
summers. (She lived with us during the school year.)
My mother's eldest sister, Elsa Sanford, still lived on
the family farm with her husband, Ken, and their five
children. My mother's other sibling, Dorthea, lived in
Ohio with her husband, Ray, and daughter, Janet.
They were my only relatives who lived more than an
hour's drive away.

My mother's great-great-grandfather, William
Cowan, came to America from Scotland in 1821 and
cleared the land in New Kingston so he could be a
dairy farmer. Family lore is that the table I was
standing beside was made from a cherry tree that was
growing on the Cowan farm at the time William
cleared the land. Family lore also has it that until
William cleared the land, it had been covered by forest
for as long as forests grew in the Catskill Mountains.

The table is made of wide boards and was in
pristine condition. It was covered with heavy white
muslin to protect it from my sticky little hands. It
resided in our large dining room against the window
that was to the left of the big dining room window that
faced Ruth Carey's large Victorian house. My father's
paternal grandfather, Howard Mayes, built Ruth's
house in 1899 and decorated the outside with lots of
gingerbread. Family records say he charged five
hundred dollars for the labor. If I stood on my tiptoes
and peered over the table, I could see Wagner Avenue
just beyond the tall spruce tree in our yard. Little did I
know that in a few years the pine tree, as we called it,
would be one of my favorite places to play.

My father's parents, Victor and Nellie Mayes,
purchased our Victorian house around 1928, when my

father, Murray, was nine. They bought it from a Mr. Harris. Mr. Harris left behind a very tall hall mirror, which resides in my home today; a plant whose offshoots I have; and a top hat, which I can't find. Grandma Mayes lived half a mile down Wagner Avenue, beside my father's veneer mill. My father's only sibling, Geraldine Cantwell, lived across the street from the mill with her husband, Jim, and her son, Danny.

I nearly always played on the floor in the dining room because, other than the laundry room, that was the sunniest room. The living room was dark because the roof of Mr. Harris's famously extravagant porch kept the sun out. The porch went along the whole front of the house and halfway around one side. On numerous occasions, Grandma Mayes told me the village talked about Mr. Harris's two-thousand-dollar porch for years.

My mother must have liked having me in the dining room because this is where my wooden, white-and-gray-oilcloth-covered toy chest resided. And, since I never liked to be far from my mother, the dining room was fine with me. I could easily find her no matter what downstairs room she was in.

For several days, Mother had been telling me that she was going to have a baby in a few weeks. Mother was a registered nurse and, always wanting to do the right thing, had been reading Dr. Benjamin Spock's *Baby and Child Care* about when to tell a three-year-old child a sibling was going to enter the house.

"Is the baby going to be a boy or a girl?" I asked her each time we had this conversation.

"I don't know," was the reply.

"I want a brother."

"Well, I can't promise you a brother," Mother said. Always be truthful, that was one of Mother's mottoes.

After these conversations, I wandered over to the cherry table and looked out the window. I studied the blue sky and watched the very tall pine tree gently move in the breeze.

"Please send me a brother," I said to God over and over again. I thought, *If God is paying attention, certainly He will send me a brother.*

Finally, at the end of July, the baby was born. It was a boy! I was elated. I remember concluding that talking to God and hoping as hard as anyone can is what produced my brother, Brian. Mother just didn't understand how these things really work.

Brian was a happy baby. Mother loved playing with him in the morning. As the morning passed, she would look at the kitchen clock and say, "I know I should be doing my housework, but he is so good-natured and so much fun in the morning."

Three and a half years later, my mother was pregnant again. I didn't care whether the baby was a boy or a girl. I was open to either. So, while I knew how all of this worked, I didn't want to bother God again. And besides, in the intervening years He had ignored most of my other important requests, like convincing my parents to get a dog instead of a cat. So I was no longer sure He was really paying attention to me.

Chapter 2

And Then God Gave Me Dean

Dean in backyard, 1962

At the end of February 1956, my mother's Aunt Berthie came to stay with us while we awaited the birth of my parents' third child. Aunt Berthie was Bertha Koutz, the unmarried sister of my mother's mother, Anna Cowan. My mother's first name was also Bertha. She never liked her name, but she was fond of and respected Aunt Berthie.

Grandma Cowan always said, "Berthie was a beautiful young woman. She had many callers and chances to get married. But she was just too particular."

What a strange way to view the situation. I thought one either fell in love or didn't. I didn't think being "particular" had anything at all to do with it.

Aunt Berthie was reserved and old-fashioned. She certainly stood out in her sturdy black tie shoes with one-inch heels, her long white hair in a bun covered with a hairnet, and her wire-rimmed glasses. I couldn't imagine her going out on one date, much less a series of them.

Aunt Berthie lived and worked on the Koutz farm with her brother, Julius, and his wife, Louise. Since she had no pressing day-to-day responsibilities, she was the logical choice to come to take care of Brian and me when Mother went to the hospital to have a baby.

Around nine or ten in the evening of March 4, 1956, Dad came home from the hospital and told Brian and me that we had a new baby brother. [1] I asked him what the baby's name was and he said, "Dean Eric."

"I think it would sound better if his name were Eric Dean," I said. Dad smiled and told me it was too late to change it now.

In a few days, Brian, Dad, and I went to Margaretville Hospital to pick up Mother and Dean. She sat in the middle of the backseat with Dean in her lap and Brian and I sat on either side of her. (Car seats

---

[1] After Dad left the hospital, Mother started to hemorrhage. Dr. Huggins, who was our family doctor and who delivered all three of us, instructed a nurse to massage Mother's uterus, but the nurse didn't massage it hard enough. When Dr. Huggins checked on Mother a little later, Mother was barely alive because she had lost so much blood. She had several transfusions and got what at the time was diagnosed as non-A, non-B hepatitis from one of them. She was in the hospital only an extra day or two. When she was in her sixties, medicine had progressed to the point where she was diagnosed as having chronic hepatitis C. She had interferon injections, but they didn't help much. She died at the age of seventy from complications of hepatitis C. She always needed a nap and I now think it was because she was always fighting hepatitis. After she was diagnosed with hepatitis C, she said it was a good thing she had lived a healthy life style and didn't like alcoholic beverages.

for children hadn't been invented yet, and our car didn't have seat belts.) Dean slept the whole way home. I was so excited. I couldn't wait for him to wake up.

As soon as we walked into the house, Mother put Dean on a large, green hassock while she took off her coat. In a few moments, he woke up and started to cry. Mother picked him up to comfort him. It didn't help much. He cried most of the time for the next year.

"This afternoon, I took Dean to Dr. Huggins. I still wonder if he has a small blockage in his intestines or an allergy. But he has gained weight and is developing normally. Dr. Huggins said he can see nothing wrong with him," Mother said to Dad at dinner more than once during Dean's first few years of life.

"Well, I guess we'll just have to wait for him to grow out of what ever is bothering him," Dad said.

I am pleased to announce he did. Little did Mother and Dad realize that these years would be the easy part of raising Dean.

Starting in April 1959, when Dean was three, every day our doorbell rang around eight thirty in the morning. Mother would go to the door and Dean's friend Johnny, who lived a few houses down the street, was there.

"Johnny, what are you doing here?" Why she kept saying this is beyond me, but that is how the dialogue always started.

Johnny, who was a month younger than Dean, would say, "Can I come in and play?"

Mother would usually say, "It's too early to come here to play. Why don't you go home and come back later?"

Johnny would then start to cry and say, "Mommy told me to come here and not to come home until later. I tried to go back, but she locked the door."

Mother always let him in and then would send him home at lunchtime.

When Dad came home for lunch, she would say to him, "I should turn that Beverly into the child welfare authorities. It's terrible the way she treats Johnny. Now, I feel like I'm stuck raising that kid too. I feel so sorry for him. It's not his fault his mother stays out all hours of the night and drinks and then sends him here when he gets up."

When winter arrived, it was sometimes below zero when Johnny rang the doorbell. While he lived only five houses down the street, the fact his mother sent him out in extremely cold weather made Mother mad. But she always let Johnny in and never called the child welfare authorities.

Finally, summer came. Dean was four and he started to explore the neighborhood, mostly on foot, but sometimes on his tricycle. Mother had established boundaries: We could go up Wagner Avenue to the telephone pole just past Ruth Carey's house and down Wagner Avenue, past three houses, to the white fence. Mother explained to us that she could easily see us from inside the house if we stayed within this territory. Under no circumstances could we cross the street.

Brian and I followed the rules without question. If Mother said these were the rules, that's all there was to it. If I wanted to visit my best friend Dick, who lived just past the telephone pole, I had to get permission from Mother.

Dean, on the other hand, challenged every rule. That summer, he nearly drove Mother over the edge. He commonly rode his trike or walked all the way down to his friend Johnny's house, two houses past the white fence, or up to the Park Terrace Hotel pool, three houses past the telephone pole, just to watch the summer visitors (mostly ladies in their seventies and eighties speaking Yiddish) swim and sunbathe.

"Mom, can I ride my bike on the porch?" Dean frequently asked.

"Yes. But promise me you'll stay on the porch," Mother said.

"I will. I promise," Dean always said.

Mother then continued doing laundry or the dishes until she realized she hadn't seen or heard Dean for a while. She would go out to the front porch to look for him. Sometimes he was still on the porch just watching the activity on the ballpark, which was across the street. But, all too often, he was nowhere in sight. If his tricycle was also missing, Mother would say, "Darn him. He knew darn well his bike wasn't on the porch."

Fortunately, there was a very good chance he was simply riding on the sidewalk or up someone's driveway and she would soon find him. If he wasn't in sight, she went to the end of our sidewalk and called his name. Frequently, there was no answer.

Mother would walk up and down the sidewalk, calling, "Dean. Dean. Where are you? Dean! Come home this instant!" with her voice growing louder and more frantic each minute.

Her heart sank if she came across his tricycle on someone's lawn or driveway and there was no Dean in sight. She would stand beside his tricycle and call, "Dean, where are you? Come here!"

Often Dean replied, "I'm right here Mom," as he walked from behind a tree or someone's garage.

When Mother couldn't find Dean after searching for about fifteen minutes, she would enlist Brian and me to help look for him. She knew exactly where we were because, perfect children that we were, we had told her where we would be.

"Marilyn. Brian. I can't find Dean. Will you go over to the ballpark creek and look for him? I'm going to take the car and drive through town and then down to the mill to look for him. I'll be back in about twenty minutes."

Usually, one of us would find him in one forbidden territory or another. But several times that summer and the next one, Mother called Dad at the mill to ask him to help find Dean. Her biggest fear was that Dean had drowned in the creek behind the ballpark or had been hit by a car on Main Street. On more than one of these occasions, Dad got two or three of his employees to join in the search.

It wasn't uncommon to find Dean throwing rocks in the creek behind the ballpark. To get there, he crossed the street in front of our house, walked all the way across the ballpark, and down an embankment. Once there, he wandered up and down the stream.

One day, the doorbell rang and I answered the door. It was Phil, a boy who was a year or two older than I. He had a reputation for being somewhat of a bully, but he never bothered me. Mother had always told us to be careful around Phil and to not get him mad at us. She said she just didn't trust him. When I pressed for details on what bad things he had done, she could never come up with any. But she was the mother, so what did I know?

"Is your mom home?" Phil asked.

"Yes. Just a minute, I'll get her," I said.

"Phil. What do you need?" Mother said.

"Can you come over to the creek? Someone threw a rock and hit Dean in the head. He's bleeding."

"Thanks so much for getting me, Phil. I'll drive right over. I really appreciate your coming to get me. Hop in the car so you can show me exactly where he is," Mother said.

Mother took some clean towels and off she and Phil went. Soon, she and Dean were back home. She had him sit in a chair in the kitchen as she carefully examined his wound. In less than a minute, she announced, "You'll be okay. You don't need any stitches."

She just bandaged him up and told him to lie down with the gray, waterproof ice bag on his head. Of course, his resting lasted all of twenty minutes.

We often wondered whether her judgment on these medical matters was correct, but she was (A) the mother and (B) a registered nurse. Whenever Brian or I questioned her judgment on matters of health, she quickly dismissed our concerns. I guess she thought there was no need to bother a doctor with such trivial matters as, oh, let's say, a profusely bleeding head wound.

"All head wounds bleed a lot. He's okay," Mother said in response to my question as to whether she should take him to the hospital.

From that day forward, Mother always said, "That Phil has gotten a bum rap. He is a nicer kid than people had led me to believe."

Just what I thought, was my reaction to Mother's new analysis of Phil.

Another favorite hangout for Dean was in front of Gale's Store on the corner of Bridge Street and Main Street. To get to Bridge Street, he simply walked past several houses, the Park Terrace Hotel, the hotel pool, and the synagogue. He then turned left, crossed Wagner Avenue, and proceeded up the sidewalk on

Bridge Street (a very short street) until, voilà, he was at Gale's Store on Main Street. Quite a trip for a four-year-old.

There was more going on at Gale's than on Wagner Avenue. Lots of people stopped in Gale's for a newspaper or to sit at the lunch counter for a cup of coffee or an ice cream soda. Gale's also had comic books, board games, toys, skis, ice skates, fishing rods, newspapers, magazines, and candy, just to mention a few of the wonders of the place. It was the perfect place for a little boy to spend some time, especially when the little boy knew nearly everyone who lived in or near Fleischmanns by name. In fact, he knew more people by name than I did.

Dean's ability to observe what was happening and the fact he knew so many people made him the perfect investigative reporter. As a result, we sometimes sent him to the scene of minor accidents or arguments so he could gather the details for us. Because of his age, no one suspected that this was his role. Then he would come home with the full story of who did what to whom.

While Dean liked the ballpark creek and Gale's, he found other interesting things to do when he was with Johnny. They spent a lot of time wandering up and down Wagner Avenue, going behind houses and garages inspecting things and creating mischief.

One day, Dean and Johnny found an open can of green paint and some brushes behind the garage of a house near where Johnny lived. Stanley Shaver had been painting the frames on some storm windows and had gone in for lunch. When he returned to his project, he found that his white garage had green swirls on it and that his front sidewalk had been beautified.

When Dean showed up at home for lunch, he had clearly been around green paint. As Mother was interviewing Dean on the front porch about his latest escapade, she noticed Stanley walking up the sidewalk in his painting clothes, looking left and right as he progressed. Mother called out to Stanley and asked him if he had been painting. Stanley told her he had and explained what he'd found when he returned from lunch.

"Well, I'm quite sure I know who the culprits are. One of them is right here. Dean, apologize to Mr. Shaver for what you and Johnny did," Mother said.

Surprisingly, Stanley wasn't terribly angry. He told Mother, "I shouldn't have left that stuff out there. It's partially my fault and I need to paint my garage anyway."

Another thing in Dean's favor was that Stanley liked Dean. Stanley read the electric meters for the power company, and from the time Dean could walk and talk, he always ran to greet Stanley and followed him to the meter in the cellar. So their friendship was quite deep, given that Dean was four and Stanley was in his forties.

When Dean returned home from his expeditions, Mother would firmly remind him where the boundaries were. He acknowledged that he knew where the boundaries were and would add one of his ten thousand very valid reasons for breaking the rules, such as, "But I just wanted to get a truck Johnny took home with him yesterday." For years, many of Dean's sentences began with, "But I just . . . ."

The summer Dean was four, he got at least one spanking every day. Seriously, I remember this. It was ridiculous. If the infraction wasn't too serious, Mother spanked him with her hand. If the infraction was serious, she spanked him with the dreaded fly swatter. (Mother was old school about corporal punishment.) By the end of the summer, I began to wonder what the point was. These spankings certainly didn't seem to change his behavior. From my perspective, spankings didn't hurt much more than my ego. So I assume this was Dean's analysis as well. I was never sure they even bruised his ego. To him, it was just another skirmish in his battle (or maybe it was a war) of wits with Mother.

During the fall and winter when Dean was four, Mother sometimes went shopping in Kingston with her good friend Sue Barrett. Brian and I were safely in school, but, of course, she had to tote Dean along. Kingston was a forty-five-minute drive away and had stores with things we couldn't get in or near Fleischmanns. So every two or three months, Mother and Sue would go to Kingston for the day. Usually Mother returned with some clothing for the family and, occasionally, takeout chicken chow mein for dinner. This was the only takeout we had growing up. Takeout hadn't yet arrived in the mountains.

Mother dreaded taking Dean on these trips. He was impossible to keep track of in the stores. For example, if Mother was looking at pants to determine if they would fit Brian, she would say to Dean, "Stay near me while I look at these pants. Don't go out of my sight. Do you hear me?"

Dean would reply, "Okay, Mom."

In a minute or two, Mother would look up from the pile of pants and Dean would have disappeared. She would stop what she was doing to go look for him. Sometimes, he was just behind a nearby clothing rack and sometimes he had wandered half a store length away.

Finally, she got the brilliant idea of giving Dean a dollar and leaving him all alone in Woolworth's department store. The Woolworth's in Kingston had several aisles of three-foot-high wooden tables with three-inch sides to contain all of the treasures on the tables. Dean could barely see onto the tables. He walked up and down the aisles and peered at all that was for sale. How should he spend his dollar? There were cars, trucks, plastic men, water pistols, cap guns, rolls of caps, paddles with balls tied to them with an elastic string, tic-tac-toe games, jacks, marbles, etc.

Every half hour or so, Mother would go to Woolworth's to make sure Dean was still there. He always was, fully engrossed in deciding how to spend his dollar. Finally, everyone was happy! In later years, Mother said she was sure the child protection authorities wouldn't have approved of her leaving him all alone in Woolworth's. But, she said, "It made us both happy."

Once Dean was no longer a baby, Mother and Dad would occasionally take the whole family on vacation. These vacations were usually from Friday afternoon through Sunday afternoon, because Dad always felt he couldn't be away from the mill for long. If these vacations were during the school year, they would pick us up at school around noon on Friday. Legally, we were truant . . . something no one ever mentioned, even though Dad was on the school board most of the years I was in school.

The fall Dean was five, we went to the Red Lion Inn in Stockbridge, Massachusetts, for the weekend. Stockbridge was then, as now, a quaint New England village. We kids had one room and Mother and Dad had a connecting room. On Sunday morning when we returned from breakfast, Mother went into our room to pack our clothes. Soon I heard her say in a rather loud voice, "Dean, did you do this? Murray, can you come in here?" So, of course, Brian and I stopped what ever we were doing and came to look as well.

There was Mother pointing at the wallpaper behind the door. Dean had taken her lipstick and scribbled on the wall.

"Well, I guess the next step is to tell them at the front desk. We'll offer to pay to have the room repapered. That is all I know we can do," Dad said.

"I should have kept better track of my lipstick. It never occurred to me he would do something like this," Mother said.

The hotel staff were very understanding, and the manager said he was quite sure there were extra rolls of the paper in the attic. A few days after we returned home, Mother received a call from the Red Lion Inn reporting that they had indeed found enough spare paper to fix the wall.

Needless to say, Mother couldn't wait for Dean to start school. She needed a break from the 24/7 job of trying to supervise him.

Once Dean started school, Mother and Dad were often on his case to improve his grades. He didn't misbehave in school, but he didn't like to do his homework. When he was in grade school, Mother imposed the No TV Until You Have Finished Your Homework rule on numerous occasions.

One day after looking at Dean's report card, Mother again announced the No TV Rule, effective immediately. For some reason, the rule never bothered me, even though I wasn't the cause of it. At the time, Dean was in the habit of watching whatever movie was being shown on TV at four in the afternoon. He immediately protested. "I want to watch the movie.

They've advertised it all week and I really really want to watch it."

"What's the name of the movie?"

"Monster on the Campus."

"Well, okay. But this is the last movie."

And so it went. I never understood why Mother caved in. Her age must have gotten the better of her. She never would have caved when Brian or I were that age if we had had such poor grades.

Things improved only marginally as Dean grew. When he was in fifth grade, a girl brought some small chocolate candies to school and dared Dean and one of Dean's good friends to eat a few. He ate six and his friend ate two. Considering that Dean doesn't like chocolate, it is a mystery why he ate any.

Well, by evening, neither boy was feeling very well. Dean's friend missed one day of school because of a "stomach bug" and Dean missed two days.

Several days later, Mother, ever the detective, asked Dean if he had eaten anything unusual before he got sick. Dean then confessed that he and his friend had eaten a candy called ex-lax.

All Mother said was, "I hope you've learned your lesson."

Mother frequently knew what had happened in school before we got home because she had friends who worked at the school. But Mother never let on that she knew things. She just tricked us into giving full confessions or fully reporting all events.

Mother had rules about what road we could take when walking the three-quarters of a mile to and from school. We had to stay on Wagner Avenue and go over the hill. Mother thought it was too dangerous for us to go on Main Street. I was never sure what she thought was dangerous about Main Street, but that was her rule. We always walked to and from school over the hill. It was a tad shorter than going on Main Street. Mother told Brian and me that we could come home via Main Street when we got to sixth grade.

Well, I got to sixth grade and started to come home via Main Street. Two years later, Brian sought and got permission to come home via Main Street even though he was only in fifth grade. So much for rules.

But the killer was: Next thing I knew, Dean—who was in second grade—was walking home from school on Main Street, without Mother's permission. Brian and I would complain and Mother would lecture Dean. He would say, "But I just want to walk home with my friends." Note the use of one of his famous "But I just . . ." sentences.

He would walk home over the hill for a day or two and then he would be back to using Main Street. Mother gave up on this battle. Some things in life are worth fighting over and some things aren't.

As Dean knew from being at Gale's, there was a lot more action on Main Street than on Wagner Avenue, especially the portion of Wagner Avenue that went over the hill to school. Also, his reports of what he saw on his trips home from school were more informative than either Brian's or mine.

Dean's well-known powers of observation were confirmed one day when Mother made Dad's favorite lunch—soup. This batch happened to be vegetable beef soup, one of Mother's specialties.

"Be sure to add the drippings that are in the bottom of the broiler pan after broiling steak or London broil and some turnips," Mother always explained to me when I complimented her on her vegetable beef soup. "That's what gives my soup such a hearty flavor with a little snap. Then, be sure to add a bay leaf or two, and some oregano, parsley, sage, and thyme."

Dean was hungry for lunch around eleven thirty, so Mother gave him a bowl of soup.

"Mom, this soup has bugs in it," Dean said as he was stirring it to cool it off.

"Oh, it's just your imagination. You see the spices floating around," Mother said.

A little after noon, Dad came home and Mother dished him up some soup. "Bertha, this soup has bugs in it," Dad said.

"That's just what Dean was trying to tell me. Let me take a look," Mother said as she peered into the kettle.

"My goodness. Dean was right. There are bugs in the soup. They must be in the flour I used as thickening. Guess I'll have to throw it out. That's really too bad. It smells like one of my best soups in a long time," Mother said.

After lunch one fall day, Mother was in the back room of the attic putting away summer clothes and pulling out winter ones. Our out-of-season clothes were stored in custom-built cabinets with large wooden drawers that didn't slide at all well.

As Mother shook the winter items looking for moth holes in the wool clothing, a few stray mothballs always landed on the floor. As a result, whenever Mother was changing our clothes for the season, the whole attic smelled of mothballs. She was always engaged in a pitched battle against moths. Some years, Mother was in the lead and other years, the moths won a skirmish or two. If polar fleece had been invented, I'm sure we would have owned plenty of it.

The back room of the attic also had a large, old-fashioned wardrobe closet. It held a few hanging items, like Mother's beaver coat. The closet had only one shelf, at the top. That is where Mr. Harris's top hat usually resided.

Dean bounded up the attic stairs. "Mom, look what I found!" he said excitedly, holding out his hand with a perfect two-foot long, transparent snakeskin in it.

Mother was silent for a moment and then let out a yell followed by, "Oh Dean. Get that out of here!"

She was pale and had to sit down to compose herself.

Dean was sure he was going to have to call someone for help. But Mother recovered in a few minutes.

She was always embarrassed by her fear of snakes. Though she tried not to let us kids know just how afraid she was, she never succeeded in disguising it despite her best efforts. She said her fear came from unexpectedly finding big milk snakes in the woodpile as a child.

Starting in eighth grade and throughout high school, Dean did a lot of backpacking on the nearby trails that traversed the mountains. He went in all seasons and developed a lot of skill and confidence in his ability to survive the elements in the winter.

His love of sleeping outdoors started when he was four. For many summers, all of us would sleep on the front porch with our older cousin Elaine, one of Aunt Elsa's children. On warm summer evenings, we would drag the lawn chairs from the backyard to the front porch, line each one with three blankets, bring down our pillows, and wrap up. We slept some and shivered some because it nearly always got quite cold by dawn. It always seemed that just when I finally fell sound asleep, the milkman would wake me as he put milk in the container on the porch.

Dean loved to go camping with his friends. Whether this was from his love of sleeping outside or the shenanigans that he and his friends, one of whom was our minister's son, got in to when they went camping is an open question.

Of course, Dean and his friends smoked cigarettes and cigars on their camping trips and in the church basement, since it was right beside the parsonage. Starting at the age of twelve, Dean bought his cigarettes at Gale's. He was always amused when Mother sent him to Gale's with a note authorizing him to buy cigarettes for a guest who needed some. *She's so clueless*, he thought. *She has no idea they sell me cigarettes on a regular basis without a note.*

Then, of course, there was alcohol. Where could a fourteen-year-old get that for his camping trips? But this was no problem for Dean.

One day, Dad said to Mother at dinner, "Have we been giving away a lot of liquor recently? There doesn't seem to be as much in the attic as I thought."

Dad bought his liquor by the case from Sid Silverstein, the owner of the liquor store on Main Street. Every so often, he bought a case of Scotch and a case of Canadian Club whiskey. In the summer, he would ask Mother to have Dave Solomon, the owner of one of the local grocery stores, deliver one or two cases of whatever beer was on sale, but beer wasn't the subject of this discussion.

Dean sat at the table waiting to see what would happen next. He was thinking, *I guess it isn't a good idea take two bottles in one week. I really regret taking that second bottle after dropping a bottle on the sidewalk in front of Ruth's house. I thought I was*

holding it very tightly under my jacket as I was
walking up to the church to hide it for next weekend's
camping trip with Rick. But it just slipped.

As luck would have it, Mother said, "Well, I
remember taking a bottle up to Uncle Charles's the
last time we went and I think we gave some to Sue and
Charley as a thank-you gift."

"Guess that explains it," Dad said.

Whew, that was close, Dean thought.

Dean became so enamored of camping that he
took up winter camping. And, between the ages of
thirteen and nineteen, instead of sleeping in his bed,
he slept on a cot on the balcony, unless it was
extremely cold. He also turned off the hot-water
radiators in his bedroom, so it too would stay
extremely cool.

One Christmas Eve, the weather forecast was
for temperatures of twenty or more degrees below zero.
Our parents told Dean to turn the radiators on in his
bedroom because they didn't want them to freeze
during the night. Dean went upstairs and turned on
his radiators. Dad then turned up the thermostat so
they would get warm. Well, they didn't!

Upon further investigation, the water in an
elbow in a pipe had frozen. If the radiators in Dean's
room were on, the pipe took hot water to the radiators.
If the radiators were off, the water just sat in the pipe.
The pipe was located in a very cold, inaccessible, part
of the cellar. Dad tried to find a plumber who was
home, but couldn't locate one. It was Christmas Eve,
after all.

Dean had "tinkered" in plumbing some, so he
told Dad he could replace the elbow. While Dad wasn't
the least bit handy in the carpentry or plumbing
worlds, for some reason we always had tons of spare

parts on hand for nearly every occasion. Having no choice but to rely on Dean, Dad let him replace the frozen elbow. Of course, this required the use of a blowtorch.

On more than one occasion, Dean saw smoke emanating from the very dry floor joist near the elbow. But, much to our parents' amazement and joy, he replaced the elbow. Both he and Dad got up during the night and went to the cellar to make sure there was no fire.

So, while Dean could sleep on the balcony until hell froze over, from that day forward, he had to keep his bedroom at a decent temperature.

Dean no longer sleeps outdoors. He is married with children, grandchildren, and a home of his own.

After we were grown, when people asked Mother how many children she and Dad had, she usually replied, "Three. We had Marilyn and Brian, and then God gave me Dean!"

Chapter 3

My Life as a Smoker

Dean in our front yard as he looked when he
had his first cigarette, 1958

I remember my first cigarette. It was a
beautiful fall day in 1956. I was seven years old and
Brian was four. Mother and Dad had had a party the
night before. It was a Ladies Home Bureau party.
Mother was a member of the Ladies Home Bureau and
she loved going to and giving parties for those ladies
and their husbands.

I'm not sure what the Ladies Home Bureau did,
exactly, but it met monthly. After a Home Bureau
meeting, Mother would show us some craft she had
made; or, we would have some newfangled dessert or
vegetable for dinner that she had learned about at
Home Bureau. Dad was never enthusiastic about new

foods, so they didn't make a frequent appearance at our table.

When my parents had a party, we children could stay up for a little while as the guests arrived. We would greet them and then we had to go upstairs to bed. It was nearly impossible to sleep because the adults were very boisterous. Frequently we would lie on our stomachs and peer down the rose-colored, wool-carpeted stairs to watch the guests, all the while hoping not to get caught spying. We seldom were. They were all too busy. We never saw anything shocking. It was mostly adults talking, drinking, laughing, and playing silly games, like pin the tail on the donkey.

One morning after one of these parties, Brian and I found a cigarette pack containing four cigarettes. It was on the end table on the right side of the green sofa, near a pile of used napkins. Since neither of my parents smoked, we weren't sure what to do. We took the pack to Mother and asked if we could smoke the cigarettes. She said, "You can smoke them. But you must light the match in front of me and smoke them where I can see you. I don't want you kids burning the house down."

With that, we were off to get some matches and start smoking. Being very inexperienced smokers, we didn't inhale. Who would ever want to do a nasty thing like that? We didn't especially like the taste of the smoke, but we did hold it in our mouths and experiment with the various ways one can blow smoke out of the mouth and/or the nose. We never got the smoke to come out of our ears, though Lord knows we tried.

After that, we looked forward more than ever to the parties our parents gave, and afterward always went on a search for abandoned cigarettes. We usually found one or two on an end table or buried behind a couch cushion. As we became more experienced smokers, we tried to make smoke rings, like the caterpillar in *Alice in Wonderland*. But we never really got the hang of it.

The summer I turned nine, Brian and I found three perfect cigarettes after a party. What luck! They hadn't been dropped in a drink, didn't have lipstick on them, and weren't crushed. Our Mother was outside with Dean who, at two and a half, was learning to ride a tricycle on our sidewalk. Dean was clad in just a T-shirt and a cloth diaper held together with very large safety pins that were made especially for diapers. Brian and I got a book of matches and, as was our custom, ran up to Mother seeking permission to light up. Dean pestered Mother to let him have one. Brian and I protested that he was too young, but to no avail. Mother said, "Oh, you two need to learn to share."

Not only was Dean no good at lighting a cigarette (Brian had to help him with the match), but he drooled out the cigarette before he had smoked half of it. Of course, now that it was soaking wet, neither Brian nor I was interested in it, even if it might dry out. So there, thanks to Mother, was a ruined treasure.

"Mom, he's ruined a perfect cigarette. I mean, it was perfect," I said.

"I told you not to let him have one," Brian said.

"I'm sorry. Next time he'll be a little bigger and this probably won't happen," Mother said.

Of course, now that we were becoming experienced smokers, what were we to do between parties with no abandoned cigarettes in the house? Our yearning to smoke usually struck us most strongly on Sunday afternoons when our parents were reading the paper, listening to music, or napping. Put simply, we were bored.

Our father had smoked a pipe for a year or two after college, and his old pipes were in a wooden end table that had a hinged door. There were two pipes on the top shelf, way in the back. We frequently got the pipes out and took them to the laundry room sink. We started out trying to make soap bubbles by mixing dishwashing soap with water and putting it in the pipes. We poured the soapy water into the bowl of the pipes and blew our hearts out. We seldom got a bubble. The soapy water would flow down the mouthpiece into our mouths. The taste was horrid: stale pipe smoke and soap. We would spit the stuff out, wipe our mouths off, and, on rare occasions, even brush our teeth.

The idea for our next experiment came from our father. He often had suggestions that would keep us busy. He said to try corn silk in the pipes. We did. Our first attempt was an utter failure because we didn't know enough to dry the silk. The next attempt was much more successful. We dried the corn silk on the back porch on a newspaper. Success! Dried corn silk burns very well, maybe too well for our purposes. On the one hand, you need a ton of it because it burns very fast. On the other hand, you can't smoke it for long because it's very hot. The smell isn't too bad and the taste is only half bad. Our conclusion was that corn silk was an okay substitute for a real cigarette in the summer, if you could ignore the heat for a minute and forget what a real cigarette was like.

Then winter would set in. Although winters in the Catskills were long and cold, we enjoyed them. But they presented a problem on the smoking front. What could we smoke now that there was no fresh corn from which to get corn silk? In going through the cupboards and drawers in the kitchen and laundry room, we found a ball of short pieces of white cotton grocery twine! It was "stringy" and, with a little imagination, looked a little like corn silk. Why not? Plus, there was an unending supply, since Bussy's grocery store, where Mother did the shopping, used it to tie up her boxes of groceries.

We sought and received permission to try it. Well, string burns more slowly than dried corn silk and we sure had a lot of it. Those were the characteristics string had going for it. But it was hot and didn't taste good. Try as we might to acquire a taste for string, we just couldn't develop a fondness for it.

As we grew older, Brian and I had several smoking clubs in the icehouse. The icehouse was a white clapboard building in the back of the backyard that in olden times held ice for what our Grandma Mayes referred to as an icebox, the forerunner of today's refrigerator. Our parents had a second floor installed in the icehouse so we kids could play up there. It was the perfect place for our smoking clubs.

The membership of our smoking clubs was by invitation only and, of course, their existence was "top secret." The clubs usually had five or six kids, and one of the most important aspects of any successful smoking club from our perspective was that a few of the members have parents who smoked. They were the ones assigned to procure the cigarettes. Brian and I could round up matches and we provided the clubhouse, which came with great cubbyholes for hiding cigarettes. Not that either of our parents ever ventured up to the second floor.

We usually didn't invite Dean to be a member. I think it was because we still viewed him as too young, especially when it came to smoking. Then, one fateful day, Dean found the club in the middle of a meeting, all of us smoking away. He turned us in! Maybe we had a premonition that this might happen.

We had broken smoking rule number one: Always smoke in front of Mother. She gave Brian and me a choice of punishments, and we selected being grounded for a week. Years later, Mother said that punishment was harder on her than on us.

Mother was a good friend of all of the mothers of the kids who were at our meeting that fateful day. As we were assembling in the backyard, Mother said to all of the delinquents in her most serious voice, "I'll leave it up to you as to whether to tell your mothers about this. I'm not going to. I'll leave it up to your conscience."

Needless to say, none of them told their mothers until they were in their twenties. Brian and I never smoked cigarettes after these experiments. We both thought the whole thing was silly. Dean smoked in high school and for quite a few years after that. Now he too no longer smokes. I hasten to add that I am five nine and Brian and Dean are both over six feet tall. I wonder how tall we would have been if our parents hadn't let us smoke tobacco, corn silk, and string as children.

Chapter 4

Youth Sports

Dick standing behind me and Brian, 1958

It was early afternoon on the third Saturday of April 1958. The doorbell rang and I answered. There was Dick Pultz, my best friend since I was old enough to have friends. I had spent my whole life playing with Dick. When I was very young, our favorite activity was digging to China. When we hit the pipe that carried the sewage from my house to the cesspool, we knew we had gotten somewhat closer to China, that far away land. We always had the hose going full bore so we could wash our shovels and make great mud. By 1958 we had outgrown digging to China and baseball, football, and tag had become our all-consuming activities.

There he was on the front porch with its barn-red painted floor, standing at the front door, chewing gum a mile a minute, blowing and snapping bubbles. He had a well-worn baseball glove on his left hand and was tossing a hardball into it with his right. He was eleven years old, three years older than I.

As I approached the door, I paused for a second taking in the oval stained-glass window that was beside the front door. Nearly every house on Wagner Avenue had a stained-glass window by its front door, and I always enjoyed looking at the colored glass.

"Hey Mare, let's play baseball. Opening day was a few days ago, ya know." Dick always called me Mare. He and his dad are the only people who have ever called me that.

"Sure. Let me get my glove and the bats."

"Yippee! I'll go see who else I can find," Dick said. "You get Brian."

I knew Dick was right about this being the start of the baseball season. Dick knew everything about sports and usually anything else that was important to know. Just ask him.

Dick was viewed as an authority on sports because he had tons of baseball cards that he studied religiously, and he was the oldest of our small gang of kids. Also, his father was an avid sports fan who listened to baseball games on the radio every Saturday afternoon, whereas our father could hardly name a baseball team. He listened to the Metropolitan Opera on Saturday afternoons.

Another indication of the high esteem in which everyone held Dick was the fact he held a high office. He was the president of the girl-haters club, of which I almost became an honorary member because he once gave me the secret password.

Baseball was always played in our backyard because it was very flat and just the right size. Also, a bathroom and drinking water were a few steps away. The bases were about thirty feet apart and home plate was only a few feet from the back door, just beyond the patio. First base was a good twenty feet from the fence that separated our yard from the house owned by the Towels, an Orthodox Jewish family who were in town only during the summers. Second base was almost as far out as the middle of the yard, and third base was a good thirty to forty feet from our driveway. Fly balls hit into the hemlock hedge at the far end of the yard were automatic home runs and almost never happened. Grounders hit under the hedge were doubles.

On a good day during the school year, we could usually find about eight kids to play. In the summer, three or four more kids were available because they spent their summers in town.

As I bounded up the stairs from the first floor and rounded the corner to open the door to the attic stairs, I called out to Brian, who was five, "Come on, Brian—Dick wants to play baseball! Help me get the gloves, bats, and balls." Brian was in his room playing with his Matchbox cars.

"Just a minute," Brian said. "I want to park all of my cars in a row." A typical Brian response. He always seemed to need one more minute to do something.

I knew the baseball equipment would be in either the front or back room of the attic, never in the middle room. The bats were stored in an old glue barrel Dad had brought home from the mill. The barrel was about three feet tall and twenty inches in diameter. It was perfect for storing bats. The balls were invariably in the bottom of the barrel and the gloves were usually near the top, where the jumble of bats prevented them from descending into the depths of nowhere. We had three hardballs and one softball. We never, ever used the softball. Softballs didn't go very far and were for sissies. All true-blue baseball players know that. I found the barrel in the front room.

I got my first baseman's glove, a hardball, and my favorite twenty-two-inch bat. I also grabbed a bigger bat that some of the kids liked, as well. I put Brian's glove and two other hardballs in a pile on the floor for Brian to bring down.

As Brian and I were assembling the equipment on the patio, Dick appeared with more players.

"Okay, guys. Marilyn, Danny, and Richard are a team. Brian, Linda, and I are a team, and Mickey, you are the designated catcher for a few innings. Marilyn, odds or evens?"

"Odds," I said, as usual. "One, two, three—shoot."

We both shot out our right index finger. "Evens. I win," Dick said while laughing to irritate me. "We'll bat last. Marilyn's team is up. I'll pitch for our team. Linda, you play first, and Brian, you play second and outfield."

Dick always thought he was a great pitcher. But sometimes he let Joe pitch because Joe was a lefty. Dick thought having a lefty pitch would confuse the opposition. He failed to take into consideration that Howie, another popular pitcher, was also a lefty. So we were accustomed to left-handed pitchers.

"I think I should bat first. Danny, how about batting second and Richard, you'll bat third. That way, I'll bat fourth," I said to my younger teammates. Every team's strategy was to have the best batter bat fourth, just in case bases were loaded. We never took into consideration that with just three team members, there would be no fourth person to bat.

After three outs, my team went to the outfield. I was the first baseman because I couldn't throw from the outfield to home plate. As much as I played baseball, I didn't have a good arm. I was a good hitter, but I still threw like a girl. I was also very good at catching. So I usually played first base. At my urging, my mother bought me a first baseman's glove to go with my exalted status. This more or less assured me of that position. The only person who regularly bumped me out of playing first base was Howie. But he was in town only in July and August; so my position was secure most of the year.

The games lasted all day. There were appropriate breaks for meals, and one team member or another was always being called home to do something. As a result, Dick was always rearranging the teams.

"We have to start at zero–zero now that Linda and Richard are gone," Brian said.

"That's not enough of a change. The score is still eight to six," Dick said. Then, looking around at the disorganization before him, he moved a few players around. After Dick made the big executive decisions, he said, "Batter up. Mickey, that's you. Brian, hustle out to second base. "

Even though we lived across the street from the village ballpark, we never played ball there. As impressive as it was, its regulation-size field was too big for us, and it was too far to a bathroom and to drinking water.

Just about the only thing my father knew about baseball could be summed up in two sentences. Fact one: In the 1920s, professional teams played baseball on the ballpark. Fact two: Honus Wagner played there. "Honus who?" you ask. Well, he was one of the most famous baseball players ever. So famous that they named the street we lived on after him.

One summer day when I was thirteen, while sitting in the wicker rocking chair on our front porch, I looked up to see a baseball game being organized at the ballpark. The kids playing were a lot older than I. It was all boys and they were in high school or older. Clearly they had been planning this for some time.

One of the boys on the field was one of our local geniuses: Ian. Ian was three years older than I, and all I really knew about him was:

• he was very very smart,
• he loved meteorology and collected local weather data using a rain gauge and everything,
• he was the scorekeeper at the high school basketball games, and
• he whistled everywhere (and I mean everywhere) he went.

Eventually all of the players arrived and the teams were established. Then, the next thing I knew, all of the players were standing at attention and Ian was whistling "The Star-Spangled Banner." When he was done, there was a cheer, and then I heard, "Play ball!" Professional baseball had returned to Fleischmanns, if only in my imagination.

Usually in early October, around the time of the World Series (which, in those years, was always played during the day and the Yankees usually won), Dick declared that it was football season. Time to put away the baseball bats and gloves and to get out the football. This too was played in our backyard.

Football season was usually very short in Fleischmanns because it got dark early, and by early

November it was too cold to play. Most of our games were in the afternoon or on weekends.

We played tackle football and I was often a receiver. Dick always seemed to be the self-designated quarterback, and he always was calling for a huddle where he would mumble what his magic number would be before he yelled, "Hike!" There was usually so much confusion on the field that few of us could hear his commands, but the game would proceed apace nevertheless.

It was early October 1960 and we had just started to play football. My team had made a touchdown. Everyone on my team yelled, "Suckers take the walk!" This meant that the team that failed to defend the goal now had to walk the distance of our backyard to receive the kick and to defend the other goal.

"Mare, you're the kicker," Dick said. He then tossed the ball to me and said, "Hey, everyone watch this."

I tossed the ball and as it came down, I gave it a mighty kick. The ball sailed forever.

"Way to go Mare!" Dick said with his jaw dropping, yet again. "What's your secret?"

No one, including Dick, could kick farther than I could. When I kicked the ball, it sailed farther than anyone had ever kicked it before, at least in our backyard.

"I've been practicing," I said.

"No. Tell me," Dick said.

A week or two went by and, for obvious reasons, I was always the designated kicker for my team. Finally, one day, Dick said, "Oh come on, Mare. Where did you learn to kick like that? Summer camp?"

"Okay, I may as well tell you," I said. "Come over here and step on my toes."

"Wow, Mare. What kind of shoes are these?" Dick said.

"Steel toed. I ordered them from a catalog at the mill," I said. "I got them just in time for football." Then, as an afterthought, I said, "And, since they're saddle shoes, they're nice enough to wear to school."

Our school, like the neighboring schools, was too small and too poor to have a football team. In fact, our school was the smallest around. For some reason, it was called Fleischmanns High School even though most of the students weren't in high school. In most years, there were about 225 students in grades K–12. The smallest class I remember was the senior class of 1962, which had only four students. We really noticed if one or two large families moved in to or out of town, especially if the family had boys who played varsity sports. While we usually had enough boys to make a baseball team plus a few substitutes, the team seldom did very well because there were so few of us.

The big varsity sport at Fleischmanns High and all of the other schools around was basketball. We had both a varsity and a junior varsity team. Some years we had very good teams and made it to the sectionals. There is one home game I'll never forget.

After dinner one Friday night when I was in high school, I walked the three-quarters of a mile from our house over the hill to see the game at the school. It was winter and there was snow on the ground, but it wasn't terribly cold. I watched Brian play in the junior varsity game and he played well, as usual. Then it was time for the varsity game to start. I knew that two or three of our players had been home sick that week, but didn't realize how illness had literally decimated the team. We had only seven players!

The game got off to an okay start, since three or four of our starters were playing. But soon they started committing fouls, left and right. It must have been the tension of being so shorthanded. One of the starters had committed three fouls, and the coach put in a substitute. Then another starter committed three fouls, and in went another substitute. Then Fleischmanns was no longer loosing by eight to ten points—we were behind by sixteen to eighteen points.

At the start of the second half, the original starters were back on the floor. They made a few baskets, but then the fouls started again. One player committed his fifth foul and was out of the game for good. In came a substitute. Then, a second player committed his fifth foul and in came the last substitute. The buzzer rang for the end of the third quarter. We were now behind by twenty-two points.

The fourth quarter started and we were all hoping we could keep all of the players on the court. Then the unbelievable happened. A third player committed his fifth foul. Off to the bench he went. The Fleischmanns fans groaned and then shouted encouraging words to the remaining players. We had only four players on the court.

I thought to myself, *Boy, Marilyn, you certainly go to a very small school!* A few minutes later, another player committed a fifth foul, and off to the bench he went. The fans groaned as their heads fell into their hands. We played the last few minutes of the game with only three players! The coach of the other team put all of his second- and third-string players in. For some of them, this was the only chance they would ever get to play in a real (well, sort of real) varsity game.

Of course, we lost. But we didn't get creamed (a technical term).

In a few weeks, basketball season would be over and it would be April. I knew Dick would be at the front door ringing the bell, glove and ball in hand, saying, "Hey Mare, let's play baseball." And so would start yet another season.

Chapter 5

Guns in the Mountains

Me, 1956

Our father was a pacifist and our mother had been an army nurse when they married in 1948. She went into the army just after becoming a registered nurse. So, having seen some of the horrors of war, she too was a pacifist at heart.

To the extent possible, our parents tried to prevent guns, and anything having to do with guns, from being part of our culture while growing up. But, being human, there were exceptions. Here are four stories, three of which are about the exceptions.

GEORGE

It was the fall of 1960 and the doorbell rang. Dad was upstairs giving Dean, who was four, a bath. Brian and I were in the kitchen and we heard a man's loud voice ask, "Do you know where Grubs is? I need to find him. He really pissed me off. He borrowed money from me and hasn't paid me back."

Usually Dad was the parent who was out in the evening, at a school board, village board, or Rotary meeting. But this night, Mother was out for the evening. So it was just us three kids and Dad at home.

Dad, sensing George's inebriated state, said, "I don't know where Grubs is, but why don't you step inside and calm down. And, please point that rifle toward the floor. What do you need that for?"

George replied, "When I find him, I'm going to shoot him."

"I don't allow guns in my house, George. So, please, calm down and put your rifle on the dining room table," Dad said while pointing at the table. George just stood there, looking at the floor.

Upon hearing the discussion about a rifle, Brian and I went to the kitchen doorway and peered into the dining room at George. He was more disheveled than usual, but didn't seem to be mad at Dad. So, feeling safe, we went into the dining room to see what would happen next.

Both George and Grubs worked for our father at the mill and both were good workers. But they both had drinking problems, and occasionally one or the other came to our house in an inebriated state and asked Dad for an advance on their paycheck. On these occasions, Dad would say, "Are you sure this is what you want to do?" They always said, "I'm sure. Just lend me five dollars. You know I'm good for it, Murray." Dad would chuckle and then open his wallet and advance the money.

More than once, when Grubs or George came to the house to repay Dad, they would say, "Murray, next time don't lend me the money." Dad would just smile and say, "Okay."

The next time they asked for money, Dad would playfully remind them of their request and they would invariably say, "Murray, I really need the money. Please, just lend it to me this one more time." And Dad always would.

We often saw George staggering into or out of The Cat's Meow, one of the two bars in town. It was at the end of Wagner Avenue, across the street from Grandma Mayes's house. This night, he was tilting to one side more than usual and he had a five- or six-day growth of beard rather than the usual two- or three-day.

Next thing we knew, Dean came down the stairs without a stitch of clothing on. He was looking for Dad. Dean, even at age four, seemed to know everyone in Fleischmanns. Upon seeing George, he said, "What's that you got, George? A gun?"

Upon hearing this, George looked at Dean, stepped forward, and put his rifle on the table.

Dad convinced George to walk home; it wasn't far. Since Dad knew nothing about guns, he called the state police, who came and took the rifle. No charges were filed and in a day or two George got his rifle back.

A year or so later, I accompanied my mother to visit her good friend Millie. Millie and her husband Will lived near George and his wife Ellen. Mother and Millie were often working on one project or another for the annual church bazaar, and Mother always seemed to have to stop at Millie's to drop off or pick up something. These stops would usually last quite a while because they always had some news to tell each other.

One day when we dropped off some fabric at Millie's, she said, "Bertha, did you hear what George did yesterday around five o'clock?"

"No. What happened now?"

"Well, George had had a few too many and Ellen was out for a walk. When she got home, George was sitting on the sofa with his shotgun. He'd shot the TV. He told her he was trying to beat Wyatt Earp to the draw, but he wasn't fast enough. Can you imagine?"

"Good thing no one was hurt! That's all I can say. Is Ellen all right?" Mother said.

"She seems okay. Just the other day she told me she tried yet again to get George to stop drinking, but nothing seems to work."

"Yes, I know it is difficult to get a person to stop drinking," Mother said.

"Ellen mentioned again that George is always so nice to her and that he had a difficult youth. She said she just can't leave him. He has always given her whatever she wants and he works so hard."

"Yes. She told me the same thing a few years ago," Mother said.

As a lathe operator at Dad's mill, George was a highly paid and respected employee. Often, when we drove up to Millie's, George was in the yard tossing a ball to his two or three well-cared-for dogs. Ellen, in her carefully applied makeup, would be dressed to the nines. She looked rather incongruous out in the yard shouting encouraging words to George and the dogs. But they all had smiles and would give us a big wave. I always waved back, thinking, *He seems so calm and ordinary when he's sober.*

BB GUNS

When the Christmas catalogs started to arrive at the end of October, Brian, Dean, and I studied them like there was a major exam coming up. We got out a pencil, an eraser, and a pen. We ranked the toys and games we wanted for Christmas. One X meant we were sort of interested, two X's meant we liked it, three X's meant we really liked it, and lots of X's in ink with the item circled and starred meant we wanted it and weren't going to change our minds. We needed an eraser because every time we reviewed a catalog or a new one came, we modified our rankings.

For Christmas, we often got things we never asked for, such as underwear, socks, and pajamas. Surprisingly, we liked opening these gifts and trying on our new clothes. We usually got something educational but fun, too, like a small loom to make potholders or a chemistry set.

One year, Brian got a garage, the type that cars are repaired in, and Dean got a farm with lots of animals, trucks, and a tractor. No toy soldiers or war games in our house.

When Brian was nine, he started to put an X by all of the BB guns in the catalogs. After a year or two of just one or two X's, he became more obsessed and put many X's in ink, circled the guns, and put stars around them. Christmas mornings and birthdays came and went and no BB gun arrived.

"Mom, why can't I have a BB gun?" he asked.

"They are too dangerous. I'm afraid you'll put someone's eye out," Mother said.

There she goes again using blindness as an excuse for not letting me do something, Brian thought. *The very same reason she uses to make me go fishing with a safety pin instead of a fishhook. It's so embarrassing and the fish slide off of the safety pin every time I get a bite.*

"But I really want one. They don't cost that much. Look, right here," Brian said while pointing to an ad for BB guns in *Boys' Life* magazine. "I'll be careful."

Finally, in desperation, at age fourteen, Brian convinced Mother and Dad to let him have a BB gun—if he could raise the money. They were hoping this would discourage him.

Brian had seen an ad in *Boys' Life* that said if you sold a certain number of Christmas cards, one of the prizes was a BB gun. Brian got the order forms in the mail and went up and down the two principal streets of Fleischmanns soliciting orders. He sold enough cards to get his BB gun. Guess that showed them.

At first, he ordered BBs in small cardboard tubes from the Montgomery Ward catalog by filling out and mailing in the order form at the back of the catalog, along with a check from Mother. In a few months, it became clear that this wouldn't do. So, rather than drop the order form in the mail every few weeks, he convinced Mother to order BBs at the new Montgomery Ward store in Margaretville. The sole purpose of the store was to be a place for people to order merchandise and pick it up a day or two later. This new way of placing catalog orders shortened the wait for the merchandise, an important consideration for Brian.

By early summer, it was clear that the only sensible thing to do was to order BBs five pounds at a time. Five pounds lasted for months. Brian stored them in an old blue-and-gray Tetley tea tin in a cupboard in the laundry room near the back door. The tin contained a few of the cardboard tubes, so Brian could easily scoop up a bunch of BBs and then dribble them into his gun. Now everyone was happy.

Brian spent hours sitting on the steps of our back porch, shooting his BB gun at the ants and flies on the patio. I am proud to report that he became the best shot in Fleischmanns, at least with a BB gun.

GUNPOWDER

Dinnertime was when we discussed what we had done that day, what plans we had for the next day, and listened to the day's news. There was a lot of chatter and laughing. The only rule was that we all had to be quiet while we listened to the news on the radio. We listened to a show that came on at six forty-five called *3 Star Extra*. Sunoco sponsored it.

The only person who didn't have to comply with the Quiet While The News Is On rule was Margie, my favorite babysitter, who also helped Mother clean the house. She was a chatterbox and sometimes Mother invited her to stay for supper. She knew everything that was happening in town, and Mother always said her predictions about what someone would do next were uncannily accurate.

"Margie may not be the smartest person in town, but she sure knows people," Mother would say to Dad after yet another of Margie's predictions came true.

About the time Brian got his BB gun, one of us mentioned at dinner that in school that day we had learned the ingredients for gunpowder. All you need is sulfur, coal (carbon), and saltpeter (potassium nitrate).

Mother said, "I have saltpeter. I use it when I make corned beef. It keeps the beef red."

Dad said, "I bet the charcoal briquettes we use in the outdoor fireplace would be a good source of carbon. And I think my old mortar and pestle from my college chemistry lab days are in the attic."

"Where do we get the sulfur? Do you have any at the mill?" Brian asked.

"No, we don't have any," Dad said.

Then Mother said, "I'm quite sure they have some at the drug store."

"Can we go up-street now and see?" Brian said.

"They're closed. We'll check tomorrow," Mother said.

The next day after school, Mother gave Brian a small jar of sulfur that she had purchased at the Fleischmanns drug store.

At supper that night, Brian said, "Dad, do you know the recipe for gunpowder?"

"No, you'll have to look it up."

So off we went to the dining room bookcase to consult the *Encyclopedia Britannica*. There, in all of its glory, was the information we were seeking. So many grams of this and so many grams of that. We didn't have a scale that measured grams; but we were scientists. We only needed a starting point.

"Marilyn, can you type this up on one of Mom's recipe cards?" Brian said soon after finding the recipe.

"Sure," I said. So I got out our manual typewriter and a blank four-inch by six-inch index card from the back of Mother's recipe box. As carefully as possible, I typed out the very short recipe with no directions. I thought, *If it was good enough for the Chinese all of those thousands of years ago, it must be good enough for us.* I proofread the recipe and then promptly filed it under "G," right behind "gingerbread." Good organization is the key to finding things like this; my parents had taught me that.

In a few days, Brian was starting what would become a major hobby. Or, some might say, an obsession.

Initially, Brian made plain gunpowder in the kitchen, put it in a pile on a sheet of paper, and carefully took it out to the wooden picnic table on the patio. He got a one-foot length of cotton grocery twine to use as a fuse. After carefully nestling one end of the fuse in the middle of the pile of gunpowder, he ignited the fuse and ran. What a disappointment—the gunpowder just sizzled.

Next, he wrapped the gunpowder very tightly in newspaper with the fuse sticking out. This too just sizzled. The next evolution in trying to make the gunpowder more exciting involved filing down copper pipe, lead pipe, and anything else that came to mind and adding the filings to the gunpowder. The object was to see if any of these substances would make the flames different colors, like fireworks. Copper worked quite well; it made the flame green. But making the filings was a lot of work. He even tried flour, sugar, baking soda, baking powder, and powdered detergent. None of these worked at all well.

Brian got the *Thomas Register* (a multi-volume set of books with the names of businesses and what they sell) from the mill and, using the mill's stationery and signing Dad's name (with Dad's permission), ordered catalogs from several chemical supply companies. He then ordered samples of several chemicals. None of these produced stellar results, either.

By now, Dean was also making gunpowder. As they grew up, their experiments became more daring. One summer day, Brian took a nice-sized pile of gunpowder out to the patio, ignited it, and stomped on it. He got the loud boom he was after, but his leg came back up at him with such force, he thought it was going to be blown off. That was the end of Brian's big experiments with gunpowder. He had a new respect for what these ingredients could do.

In thinking about this event a few days later, Brian thought, *Mom, you sure are naive. You think gunpowder is safe but fishhooks are dangerous.*

Two years later, Dean also took a pile of gunpowder out to the patio and ignited it. He hit the burning pile with a hammer. It too made a big bang, but it splattered small amounts of burning gunpowder onto his face. Fortunately, he was wearing glasses, so no harm was done. This was his last big experiment with gunpowder.

In later years, Mother said, "I think we were awfully foolish to let you boys play with gunpowder. It's a real wonder no one was seriously injured."

Whenever I've been asked why my parents allowed Brian and Dean to make gunpowder I reply, "I have no idea. And, now it's too late to ask them."

MY SIX-SHOOTERS

For my seventh birthday, my parents gave me one gift I had been asking for and a second gift that pleased me no end. I had been asking for a pair of six-shooters with a holster so I could be like Roy Rogers and Dale Evans. The unexpected gift was a cowboy outfit: a pair of jeans, a red shirt, and a wide-brimmed hat with a chin strap. Life certainly didn't get any better than this.

I immediately set out learning how to quickly pull a gun out of my holster, twirl it around my right index finger, and then shoot it, just like on TV. I worked on this for a few days. When I was sure I had perfected it, I marched into the kitchen. "Mom, watch this," I said. I then drew the gun out of the holster, twirled it a quarter the way around, and bang—the end of the barrel hit me in the forehead.

My mother laughed and said, "Guess you need a little more practice."

I was hurt in all the ways a person could be hurt, emotionally and physically. I was so mad at my mother for laughing. Didn't she realize how serious this was? But, after a few minutes, even I had to smile a little at how right she was. I was afraid to try it again. What a lump I had.

Chapter 6

Swimming

Me and Danny, 1952

I'm not a good swimmer and I'm cautious around water, especially moving water. I can float on my back and do the sidestroke on my right side, the breaststroke, and the dog paddle. Well, I guess I can still do the dog paddle. I haven't tried that lately.

As a child, I remember thinking that if the outdoor reading of the indoor–outdoor thermometer in the laundry room hit seventy degrees, it was warm enough to go swimming. I have no idea where that idea came from. I do remember it happened one summer after a succession of days when the temperature didn't reach seventy. Hey, if it's summer, it must be swimming weather.

My first pool was a plastic, inflatable kiddie pool. That water got warm and was very pleasant to play in.

My second pool was a much larger fifteen-foot by twenty-foot plastic pool that was about two feet deep. It took more than a day to fill it with the hose and then took more than a week for the water to get warm. Brian, Dean, and I loved that pool. It was usually warm and right in the backyard, so we could go for a quick dip whenever we wanted. We were assigned two tasks to help maintain the pool. One was to use a net on a pole to get all of the grass clippings out of the water every so often. The second was to pour in a cup of Clorox every week or two to keep the bacteria count down. This is the amount Mother gave us. Heavens knows if this was too much or too little. I can only report that no one got sick from being in the pool, at least as far as I know.

Real swimming started when I graduated to swimming lessons at Lake Switzerland. I was six when I had my first lessons. Mother didn't know how to swim and she was determined that we would all learn.

Lake Switzerland was a man-made lake created by damming a mountain stream. There were two wooden cribs on the side of the lake where you went swimming. The cribs had wooden floors surrounded by a wooden railing. One crib was forty feet by forty feet and went from a depth of three feet to five feet. The second crib was twenty feet by twenty feet and it went from a depth of eighteen inches to three feet. The cribs were right beside each other. Along the front of each crib was a cement sidewalk, and at both ends of the sidewalk there were strips of grass where people sunbathed. Beside the smaller crib, there was a wide set of steps that you could use to enter the lake itself.

You used these steps if you wanted to swim to the raft that was quite a distance from the shore, or so it seemed to me.

Every once in a while, someone would hop out of a crib jumping around on one foot with the other foot bleeding.

"I got bit or something. Look!" the injured person would shout. Then, pointing to the railing of the large crib, they would say, "It happened right there— on the bottom rail."

Mrs. Cherry, the owner of the lake, would say to her teenage son, "Craig, go dive down and look for a nail. Take this hammer with you," as she reached for some iodine and a few Band-Aids.

I knew that if a cut were bleeding decently, iodine didn't sting. But for something like a scrape, you should always try to see if the person administering treatment would use non-stinging Mercurochrome instead of dreaded iodine. Mrs. Cherry's first-aid kit only had iodine.

My first swimming lessons were in the small crib. The lessons were always in the morning, when, of course, the water and air were the coldest. I was a tall, skinny kid and turned blue instantly.

"Why can't I have my lessons in the afternoon, when it isn't so cold?" I asked Mother time and time again.

"They're busy in the afternoon, selling tickets and minding the concession stand," was always the answer.

The first day of summer vacation after I completed fifth grade, I had just finished my breakfast and was thinking about what to do next, when Mother said, "I want you kids to sit down with me at the kitchen table. I have something to go over with you."

So all three of us kids trooped into the kitchen and sat down at the table with Mother. She then produced a chart. Down the left side was a list of chores and beside each chore was a list of the days it needed to be done. A typical list was:

1. Sweep the walk—Monday and Thursday
2. Make the beds—Every day
3. Vacuum paths—Tuesday
4. Thorough vacuuming (1 to vacuum, 1 to move furniture)—Friday
5. Dust dining room—Wednesday
6. Dust living room—Thursday
7. Clean bathrooms—Monday and Friday
8. Sweep kitchen floor—Every day

"I am tired of doing all the work around here, and now that school is out, I think it's high time you kids started to help. Here's a list of chores I want you to do. So, let's start filling in this chart. Since Dean is so young, he doesn't have to do as many chores as Marilyn and Brian."

"Mom, do we have to vacuum twice a week? Isn't once a week enough?" Brian said.

"No, this is what I want. And one more thing. Before you kids can go out to play or go swimming, you have to have finished your chores. Understand?"

Truthfully, these chores usually took us half an hour at most. But many days we were approaching lunchtime and the chores hadn't been done, the day was warming up, and we really wanted to go swimming. Needless to say, one or the other of us exerted a lot of pressure on whoever hadn't completed his or her chores so we could all go swimming.

Some years the lake was open and some years it was not. In the years the lake was open, Mother drove us the mile to the lake after lunch and we walked home between four and five in the afternoon.

Before leaving for the lake, Mother told us we could get some change out of the juice glass in the cupboard. We took enough money for our admission and for one or two Fudgsicles (my favorite), frozen small Baby Ruth or Milky Way candy bars, and a bottle of soda. Life didn't get any better than this.

When I was in high school, I usually swam out to the raft, sat out there in the sun and, unfortunately, dried off. Then I had no choice but to jump into the cold water to get back to shore. Boy, I wished someone would row over in the rescue rowboat to pick me up! No one ever did.

One of the frequenters of the lake was Elizabeth, from New York City. She was a tall, thin, beautiful teenager with long brown hair that she continually flicked from one side of her head to the other as she walked down Wagner Avenue with her grandmother. They were both very properly dressed in slacks and sweaters that were the latest fashion. When they went for their evening stroll, Elizabeth carefully balanced herself in her heels with her chin slightly elevated. She always gave us the impression that she thought we locals were mere street urchins. She was probably right.

At the lake, Elizabeth sat with her grandmother, read, applied wonderful-smelling Coppertone tanning lotion, and took an occasional dip. (The dangers of too much sun were unknown to us and, except for zinc oxide, no one we knew used sunscreen.) For years, she projected the image of a mature sixteen-year-old who was going on forty. On my way to the stairs to the lake, I'd check out what she was reading. *Well*, I thought, *I can read that stuff too, if I want to.*

So, I too took up reading Shakespeare, leaving the cover of my book in plain view when I went for a swim.

I also visited with friends, something I never saw Elizabeth do; and, being the big sister, I tried to keep track of Brian and Dean. But they always informed me they didn't need any supervision. I suspect they were right.

Our cousin Elaine, who is several years older than I, frequently stayed with us in the summer, especially if Mother felt we needed a babysitter because she had to work in the office at the mill. She only had to do this if Helen, the regular secretary, was ill. Mother hated being there, but if Dad really needed someone in the office, she was "elected."

Elaine was a lot of fun to be with. She was always thinking of things to do that would never have occurred to us. She loved babies and children and always thought Brian was the most beautiful little boy she knew. At least, that is what she was always telling Dean and me. So one day, when Mother was at the mill, Elaine dressed up Brian as a girl. Then we all walked down Wagner Avenue to show Mother, Aunt Gerry, and Grandma Mayes.

Mother thought it was funny, but Aunt Gerry thought it was terrible that Elaine took Brian out in public dressed as a girl. I never saw what the big deal was. It was one of the most entertaining afternoons we had had in a long time. Elaine even had him carry the little white pocketbook I took to church.

One of the summers that Elaine was with us, we three kids and Elaine were walking down Main Street on our way home from the lake. It was a summer that was unusually hot in the city, and there were so many tourists in town that it was difficult to walk three or four abreast down Main Street. The grocery stores were so busy that they all had lots of produce displayed on the sidewalk. On our walk home with Elaine, as we passed one of the grocery stores on Main Street with baskets of fruit on the sidewalk, she said, "Marilyn, I dare you to steal a peach from that basket."

"Elaine, I can't do that. What if I get caught?"

"Oh Marilyn, it's no big deal. You just put the peach in your pocket real fast. I'm sure you can do it." Then she laughed.

Elaine had never (well, almost never) steered me wrong. But something about this dare just didn't seem right. It took more cajoling to make me steal the peach.

Elaine laughed and said, "I knew you could do it."

After we were several paces from the store, I pulled out the peach and took a bite. "It's not even that good," I said. Elaine thought that was hilarious. I realized then and there that I wasn't cut out for a life of crime.

One year, when the lake wasn't open, we learned from some other kids that they were going to go swimming that summer at Locust Grove. This was just a deep pool in the creek between Fleischmanns and Arkville, near where the Locust Grove hotel once stood.

"Mom, can we go swimming at Locust Grove, too?" Brian asked.

"Let me ask your father," she said.

That evening at dinner, Mother asked Dad if he thought the creek water was safe at Locust Grove. Mother was sure some raw sewage made its way into the stream somewhere along the way. None of the villages in the area had a sewage treatment plant.

Each house had its own septic system, and Mother was never sure how good these systems were or, for houses located beside a stream, if they really even existed.

"I'm sure the water is safe by the time it gets down there. The stream is quite turbulent, and I'm quite sure the sun and oxygen have killed whatever bacteria might have been in there," Dad said.

Wow, is Dad smart! I thought. He analyzed that on the spot with scientific reasoning to back up his answer. It also helped that it was the answer we kids were waiting for.

We liked swimming at Locust Grove a lot. The water was warmer than the lake and it wasn't as deep. Since only local kids knew about the spot, it was never crowded. Mother drove us down there, took her lawn chair, her *Ladies' Home Journal, Good Housekeeping, TIME,* and *LIFE* magazines and some snacks. Other mothers did the same thing. She got very little reading done because the mothers did a lot of visiting, i.e., gossiping.

Another favorite place to swim was at our camp in Red Kill. It took about twenty minutes to get there, but it was really another world. Red Kill had a lot of dairy farms, and our camp was on a dead-end dirt road, far from any other building except for our neighbor, Mr. Persons. He was easily in his sixties, very thin, slightly stooped over when he stood up, usually had several days' growth of beard, always wore a tan porkpie hat with a dark band around it, smoked a pipe with sweet-smelling tobacco, and had yellow teeth. He went for a walk once or twice a day, spitting every once in a while.

Dad and my brothers visited him often. He loved to talk about fishing and hunting. Every time they returned from a visit, Dad said, "Boy, that place looks worse than the last time. There is no place to sit down or to put anything. Every chair, table, and counter is covered with old newspapers, magazines, and mail. I sure hope it never catches fire."

Of course, this description captured my imagination. So I was allowed to go visit Mr. Persons once or twice a summer. While Dad's description was accurate, the place was worse than I had imagined. I had never seen such piles of papers and clothes covered with dust and tobacco ashes. And the smell of pipe tobacco was everywhere.

Even though our camp had spider webs and mouse tracks a-million, it was the pinnacle of neatness in comparison. Our camp didn't have central heat and wasn't winterized, so we usually came at the end of April or beginning of May for a weekend or two, visited more frequently once school was out, and closed it up in October. Mr. Persons owned the land behind the camp and he had dammed up the stream to make a fire pond. He didn't mind if we played there.

The pond had a very muddy bottom but the water was warm. It was about a hundred yards in diameter and four to five feet deep, depending on how much rain we had had. We always wore old sneakers when we went to the pond and spent a lot of time catching orange salamanders, pollywogs, tadpoles, frogs, and minnows. Occasionally we found a snake in the woods nearby. Although the water was warm, it was often a little smelly by August because it was stagnant.

The best part of going to the pond was an ancient wooden rowboat that leaked like a sieve. It had a set of oars and still had the oarlocks.

"Marilyn, will you help me with this? Let's see if we can row this over to the other side this time," Brian said as he hauled the boat into the water through the muddy shore.

Once we got the boat into the water, we pulled ourselves up over the sides to get in. As soon as the first person was in, it started to sink. While it was easier for the second and third person to get in, the added weight only made the boat sink faster. We rowed as hard as we could to see if we could make it to the other side before it filled with water. We never could. But the boat never sank to the bottom of the pond. We were always able to get it to shore before it totally disappeared.

Then we tried having just one person in the boat and the others swimming alongside it, pushing and pulling it along, hoping this would allow us to get the boat to the other side. Nothing worked. Even if it was empty, it filled with water. But what entertainment!

In contrast to swimming and boating in a muddy pond at camp was swimming and boating at Lake Mohonk. If the mill was having a profitable year, we occasionally went there for a weekend. Our parents had honeymooned at this fabulous resort that looks like a castle, a very large castle.

The Mohonk Mountain House is just outside of New Paltz, New York, and was an hour and a half from home, provided we didn't get lost on the way. As we were backing out of the driveway, our parents discussed which route to take. Mother advocated for the back way because it was shorter. She was always sure that between the two of them we could get there without any problems. Sometimes she was right and sometimes we got lost.

The vacation really began as soon as we arrived at the gatehouse, which was a mile or so from the actual resort. A man greeted us and asked Dad if we had a reservation. We always did and Dad gave the man our last name. The man would then make a check mark on his clipboard. When I was very young, the man instructed us to get in the horse-drawn carriage for the ride up to the hotel (a hotel employee drove our car with the luggage). In later years the system evolved to getting into a hotel car, then to following a hotel car in our car, and finally to driving our own car after being told to go very slowly.

We all loved taking the water-powered elevator to the second or third story, even if our room didn't happen to be on one of these floors. The elevator, as well as everything else, moved at a slower, more gentle pace at Lake Mohonk. It was just what Mother and Dad were looking for and needed.

The waters of Lake Mohonk were crystal clear and the fish were huge. We kids were allowed a lot of freedom to come and go as we pleased. The resort had so many activities, we could barely fit them all in. We went swimming, canoeing, hiking, spelunking, and horseback riding. We had paddleboat races and sometimes hiked to Skytop (a stone tower from which one had a great view) on the Lemon Squeeze (a trail where we used ladders in narrow crevices) every day we were there. We played tennis and used the putting green. We often took a carriage ride in a horse-drawn carriage or hay wagon.

While we were busy with our activities, our parents went for walks through the gardens and sometimes up to Skytop on an ordinary trail, often stopping and sitting every once in a while in one of the numerous pagodas that are located throughout the resort.

In the afternoon, we kids nearly always joined them on the porch for afternoon tea and cookies. Mother would then tell us what time to be back to our room so we could all change for dinner. In those days, Mohonk Mountain House didn't serve liquor, so Dad brought a bottle from home and often had a cocktail on the balcony of our room before we went to dinner. In the evening, we often went to the large parlor where there was live entertainment.

Once back home, our neighbor Lucille sometimes took us swimming in one local hotel pool or another. Once or twice she took us to the pool at the Takanassee Hotel. Its pool was one of the most spectacular places I have ever swum. Lucille knew the owners of many of the local hotels and occasionally took us with her children, Linda and Richard, to a local hotel pool. Linda and Richard were just a year younger than Brian and I and we frequently played with them since they lived just two houses away. The Takanassee Hotel pool was much larger than the pond behind our camp. It was so gigantic, it had a raft in the middle. What a treat! Clean, warm water with a large section that was just right for us.

While driving us to the Takanassee, Lucille frequently said, "I'm not sure I'm allowed to bring you as my guests, but we aren't staying long."

This always made me a little nervous, but I knew we were in good hands with Lucille.

Knowing that nearly all of the tourists who came to Fleischmanns mostly spoke German, Yiddish, and/or Hungarian to each other, Linda said, "Mom, what should we do if someone talks to us? You know we only speak English."

"Don't worry. I can fake Hungarian," Lucille said.

And I saw her fake it more than once. She always seemed to make herself understood.

Surprisingly, on one occasion even our basement at home was a swimming hole, of sorts. In the spring, if it rained a lot and there was still snow in the mountains, the creek on the other side of the ballpark would rise dramatically. If we could see the turbulent water from our front porch, it meant that soon we would have water in our basement. That meant that Dad had to remove the circulator from the oil-fired furnace, and the house would cool down because we would have no heat. Every hour or two, we kids just stood on the cellar stairs to watch the water rise and to see what was floating around. Usually, there was an oil slick from the furnace, some wooden boards, and a cigarette butt or two from when a plumber or electrician had been to the house.

Then, one summer, there was a large storm. The cellar was seriously flooded. The water was about three feet deep and it was warm. What luck! Our own private indoor pool.

"Mom, can we put on our bathing suits and go swimming in the cellar?" Brian asked.

"Okay, just watch out for nails. I don't think there is any broken glass," Mother said.

Once in the cellar, we found an old wooden door. It made a great raft. The largest room of the cellar had a supporting wall in the middle. So we took turns paddling our newfound raft around and around the cellar. Even Linda and Richard, whose father was a medical doctor, received permission to swim in our cellar. Usually the water receded as quickly as it came, so we had our indoor swimming pool only for a day or two.

The closest Brian, Dean, and I came to drowning was the time we went swimming in Dry Brook with Elaine. Dry Brook is a rural community of widely scattered homes and farms a few miles from Fleischmanns. Jay Gould's descendants (yes, the famous Jay Gould you read about in American history class) owned (and may still own) quite a bit of land in Dry Brook along the Dry Brook stream. The land is well posted with No Trespassing signs, but nearly every local teenager has ignored these signs at least once, especially on hot days.

Elaine, the instigator of many of our misadventures, had her driver's license and a car. She told us she knew exactly where the best swimming holes were in Dry Brook, so off we all went. The stream cascades down the mountain from one deep pool to the next, through narrow rock channels. It's really one long waterfall with a few interruptions. Elaine parked the car at the place she thought was the spot where everyone went swimming.

We got in the water and swam around a little. We were the only ones there, but it looked like the right place to Elaine. The next thing we knew, the stream carried Brian to the edge of the pool and down the chute. I was next and then Dean. We all landed in the next lower pool. When I looked around, all I saw was sunlight in every direction and lots of bubbles. Which way was up? I just waited helplessly for the next event, not sure if this was the beginning of an adventure or the end of my time on Earth.

In a second or two, it occurred to me that I was lucky to be conscious. I hadn't hit my head on the way down. My attempts to swim were total failures because of the air in the water. There was nothing for my arms to push against. Soon the current carried me to the main part of the pool, and I was safe. My head popped up out of the water and I saw others swimming. This was the pool we should have been in all along. It was larger and the current wasn't as swift. We all ended up in the middle of the pool where the water was calm and then swam to shore.

"Are you guys all right?" Elaine asked from shore. She had seen us go through the chute and ran to find us, or our bodies.

"Boy, that was scary! I had no idea which way was up. The sunlight was everywhere and there were so many bubbles," Brian said. "I just watched the bubbles and when I saw some rising, I figured that way was up."

Brian demonstrated yet again the benefits of reading *Popular Science* magazine.

"How did you guys get here?" someone asked. "I didn't see you come in."

"See that waterfall?" I said. "Well, I don't recommend it as a way to get here."

Even though we had found the correct pool, we wanted to go home. We had had enough adventure for one day and learned firsthand the power of moving water.

I never went swimming in the Dry Brook stream again, and to this day have great respect for (and, more accurately, fear of) moving water.

Chapter 7

Me and My Bike

Me on my first bike at Grandma Mayes's, 1955

Freedom came when I learned how to ride my two-wheeler. Mother didn't know how to ride a bike. She never had one. And, growing up on a farm, she really didn't have a good place to ride.

"My mother always thought we were too poor for many things you kids take for granted. I never had a bike or many toys when I was a child. I just had my dolls. Living up on that farm with no other children around, they were my best friends," my mother often told me.

"Where were Aunt Else and Aunt Dort?" I asked, referring to Mother's only siblings, her sisters.

"They were older and not interested in dolls by the time I came along."

"I can't imagine being by myself all the time like that. Especially with just a few dolls to play with," I replied.

"Well, I now know that it was a bunch of nonsense. We really weren't that poor. It was all in Grandma's head. She spent a lot of money on support corsets because this and that hurt. Then they just hung in the hall closet at the head of the stairs. Her illnesses were in her head," Mother explained in a rather bitter tone of voice. "Oh well. That's past and I'm happy now."

Dad, on the other hand, was fully aware of the freedom that comes with owning a bike. Needlessly to say, it was Dad who taught me how to ride one.

I had just turned six and had gotten a two-wheeler for my birthday. It was a blue, girl's Columbia with a headlight. A large compartment that held about six D batteries powered the light.

Dad ran alongside the bike as I pedaled down our driveway and, without my knowing it, let go. The first several times I tried, I nearly fell off. But after only a day or two of Dad running beside me, I was off on my own. What freedom!

I often rode my bike the half-mile down Wagner Avenue to Grandma Mayes's and to my cousin Danny's. Once I got down there, Danny and I frequently rode up Depot Street, which was rather steep, to the Fleischmanns train station. We would park our bikes and wander around the station platform. We couldn't get into the station because it was always locked. Since passenger service had stopped a few years earlier, there were usually only four or five freight cars sitting by the station waiting to be loaded with my father's veneer.

If a freight-car door was open and the car was mostly empty, we would climb in. We were never strong enough to slide the doors. Occasionally we would climb up the ladder on the outside of a car to the roof.

"Boy, are we high up. Don't go so fast, I'm afraid I'll fall!" I said to Danny as he ran to the other end of the car toward a steering wheel.

"Come help me turn this," Danny said as he ran toward the wheel.

"What will happen if we turn it?" I said.

"It's the brake. But it is so flat up here nothing is going to happen. Come on. Help me," Danny said as he pulled on the wheel with all his might.

He was right; the car didn't move an inch.

We usually rode back down Depot Street, made a right on to Wagner Avenue, a right into the driveway that went to both the mill and Grandma Mayes's house, and then another right into Gram's driveway.

"Gram, you'll never guess what we just did," I said.

"What have you kids been up to now?"

"We just rode all the way to the train station. Do you have anything to eat?" Danny said, changing the subject so I wouldn't tell her about our climbing on top of the train cars.

Taking his lead, I never once mentioned climbing to the top of the cars.

Gram usually had something for us to eat and she was always doing a jig, as she called it, dancing around the kitchen getting our snacks out.

It was always quieter at Gram's. I enjoyed being at her house because sometimes the noise at home would get to me.

When the noise at home really got to me, I would pick up the phone, and an operator would say, "Number, please."

"Three, six, two," I replied, knowing that I could just as well say, "Grandma Mayes's, please."

"Ah-low," is the way Gram said "hello."

"Can I come spend the night?" I asked.

"Certainly. Come anytime," Gram replied.

"Okay, I'll be down after lunch."

I packed a brown paper grocery bag with my pajamas, clean underwear, a toothbrush, and my Nancy Drew mystery. I hopped on my bike and rode down to Gram's with my left hand tightly gripping the bag. While it was a short journey, it was a precarious one because the bag banged against my leg and threw me a little off balance.

Peace at last!

When I arrived, Gram was in the kitchen checking on the banana cake she made for our dessert. What a wonderful smell. She always covered it with cream cheese frosting. For years, all of us kids asked her to make us a banana cake for our birthdays. And, of course, she did. We chatted awhile waiting for the cake to get done.

Then we would have cocktail hour. If it was nice out, we would sit on her porch watching who was coming and going from the Cat's Meow, a bar that was kitty-corner from her house. Gram often had a glass of beer, poured me a Coke, and we munched on peanuts.

"I'm so glad they came out with these pony-size bottles of beer. They are just right for me," Gram told me every time we had cocktail hour.

What a neat grandmother, I always thought. *So refined, but down-to-earth.*

Gram then made dinner. She always issued me a cloth napkin. She used two napkins, one in her lap and the other beside her plate, to wipe her fingers on. She always had a nice supper for us, sometimes with homemade Parker House rolls. Gram was famous for her Parker House rolls.

After dinner, we adjourned to the living room to watch a little TV. Everything was in black and white; color TV hadn't been invented yet. She got two channels, CBS and NBC. What a treat. At home, we only got NBC.

Sometimes Danny would come over to Gram's in the evening with his father's projector. He would put it in Gram's picture window and point it at the Cat's Meow to see what the people would do now that they were in the "spotlight." Most of them ignored the light, a few waved. I always feared someone would come over to Gram's and yell at us, but no one did.

For breakfast, Gram usually had a hard roll and two pieces of bacon for each of us. She called the rolls "water rolls" because they were made with flour, water, yeast, and salt with some poppy seeds sprinkled on top. The crust was very hard and the inside was very soft. Whenever I bit into one, crumbs went everywhere. When I took my plate to the sink, my whole place mat was a mess except for the circle where my plate had been. Gram's place mat, on the other hand, hardly looked used. How did she do it? I am still trying to figure it out.

It was during these stays that I learned Gram had grown up on a farm about three miles away. She was the fourth of seven children, and her mother, Lydia Kelly Murray, died a few days after giving birth to her seventh child. Gram was nine when her mother died. Her mother went out to the outhouse to go to the bathroom soon after the baby was born. For some reason, the family always attributed her death to this trip.

Gram always said her father, James G. Murray, didn't have much of a sense of humor, but then added, "Who can blame him, with all of those children running around, and Gladys only two. No wonder Anna and Inez married so young. All I can say is that none of us ever ended up in jail."

After munching on a few peanuts and having another sip of beer, Gram continued, "Father didn't have much money. He just had a few dairy cows and had to go to the barn twice a day to milk them. I think he liked the peace and quiet there. Who could blame him?"

She added, "One summer, to bring in some extra money, the road crew boarded at our house. They were building Route 28 and needed a place to stay. Anna and Inez made the meals. Boy, could those men eat!"

I tried to fathom what it must have been like to have several strange men staying at my house while they worked on the highway. When we were away from home, we always stayed in a motel or hotel.

Gram continued, "One day, Anna made a chocolate layer cake. We kids were so looking forward to a piece of cake. We almost never had dessert. The road crew always had first choice and then the rest of us ate what was left. Well, there was about a third of the cake left, enough for all of us if everyone had a small piece, when one man said, 'Hum. Pretty big piece, but guess I can eat it.' Boy, were we kids disappointed."

"Oh, is that where Dad gets this saying from? He always says it when we ask him if he wants some dessert," I said.

"What happened to the new born?" I sometimes asked because I had forgotten this detail.

"Oh, Beatrice was adopted by Uncle Sol and Aunt Sarah. I guess Father thought he had enough to do taking care of six of us. Uncle Sol and Aunt Sarah were as poor as church mice, but such good people. We all loved Aunt Sarah. She had so many sayings. But, Beatrice was never healthy. She died young. In her thirties."

Was Gram's Aunt Sarah the source of Gram's funny sayings, I wondered? Is that why Gram said of one of her nephew's wives, "She's a horse's tail. Why, she's as much use as a fart in a mitten." I agreed with Gram's assessment of this woman based upon my few visits to her home, where clothes were strewn on every surface.

Sometimes Gram said that someone or something was "as much use as tits on a doorknob." I could just picture how useful these might be. But Gram just chattered on as if she hadn't said anything off-color or funny at all.

After commenting on how someone wasn't quite up to her standards, she would end her story with, "I better be careful what I say. You know, we are related one way or another to nearly everyone in town."

After a day or two of total peace and quiet at Gram's, I rode my bike home. While it was nice to go away for a while, it was always nice to come home.

Once home, I started right up where I had left off playing with my friends, who included kids who came to Fleischmanns for the summer. Not only did we have more players for baseball, but also the city kids introduced us to new games. One year, one of the new games was ring-a-levio.

It's a game of tag played with teams. The members of one team hide and the members of the other team look for them. Each team has a jail and puts members of the opposite team in jail by holding them long enough to say, "Ring-o-levio one, two, three."

A team can free its members who are in jail by daringly going to the jail where they are held and touching each team member in jail. But since the jail is usually well guarded, attempting a rescue can be quite tense.

The game ends when all of one team's members are in jail. At this point, a person on the winning team yells, "Olly, olly, in free," to signal to the rest of his or her teammates that it is safe to come in from hiding or searching. The losing team then stays put and counts to fifty while the members of the winning team go hide.

Many games of ring-o-levio were played until it was too dark to see. In July, these games were often interrupted because we stopped to catch lightning bugs. We usually put the bugs in a jar. Sometimes I released mine before going to bed and sometimes I brought them into my bedroom for the night. But, sadly, the next morning the bugs were no longer performing their magic. I do think most of them survived the night, however, and I released them first thing in the morning.

Some mornings, Mother would say, "Let's get some buns from Schimmerling's bakery for breakfast. Marilyn, here's some money. Will you ride up and get half a dozen?"

I only had to go up Wagner Avenue to Bridge Street, up Bridge Street, and then cross Main Street. A very short journey on a bike, and there was almost no traffic early in the morning.

Schimmerling's was a wonderful Viennese bakery. Just the smells emanating from the door made going in mandatory. The couple who owned and operated it was from Austria, I think, and had one son who was Brian's age. The first year or two, they came only for the summer. Then they decided the small rural village was the perfect place for their son to grow up. Their almond-flavored cinnamon buns were to die for. We all loved them and Mother bought them often. Her waistline suffered for it.

When her skirts and dresses got too tight, she just took them to Bertha Hubbell in Kelly Corners, a settlement about twenty-five minutes away, so Mrs. Hubbell could let the clothes out. Mother didn't wear slacks in those days. When Mother bought clothes, she always studied the seams to make sure Mrs. Hubbell could let them out. At the time, Mother thought, and I agreed, she was very smart to buy clothes with big seams. What craziness.

I loved going to Mrs. Hubbell's. She had an old-fashioned kitchen with a wood-burning stove, a windup pendulum clock that sounded on the quarter hour, a cat or two sleeping on the wooden kitchen chairs that were each covered with a braided cushion, and delicious homemade ginger or molasses cookies. No matter the time of year, it always smelled good in her house. I especially enjoyed going to see her in the winter because she had a nice fire going in the stove and it was very cozy.

She was a self-taught seamstress. In fact, even though I made my own wedding dress, Mother took me with the dress over to Mrs. Hubbell so she could make some—okay, quite a few—adjustments before the big day.

On my ride up to the bakery, I passed the synagogue. If my trip was on a Saturday morning, Meyer, the local kosher butcher, occasionally asked me to turn on the lights for the Saturday morning services. He was the rabbi. When I asked why he needed me to do this, he explained that it was against Jewish law for him to start a fire on the Sabbath. I guess this law doesn't cover us non-Jews.

Mother got most of our beef and all of our chicken from Meyer. Whenever she ordered hamburger, she ordered chuck, ground twice. What wonderful hamburger that was. Meyer's shop was small and had sawdust on the floor, which I always thought was weird. Meyer grew up in Russia, or somewhere "over there."

Meyer often had a three-day growth of beard and was very kindly. Mother explained to us he didn't have sirloin steaks and some other cuts of beef because it was against Jewish dietary laws. I was always interested in the fact that he kept chickens behind his shop, but it wasn't until I was an adult that I realized what he did with them. Mother never really discussed it. If Mother wanted chicken for dinner, she would call him in the morning and he delivered the chicken in the afternoon.

"I don't know why he can't take more time removing the pinfeathers. If his chicken weren't so good, I'd get them someplace else. I have complained to him and the last two chickens weren't bad. But this one is horrid," Mother said as she got out her candle and matches to sear the pinfeathers that were still on a chicken. Burning hair. What a horrid smell.

I usually rode my bike uptown only if I had a reason to go there. There was too much traffic and too many people on the sidewalk. While the year-round population of Fleischmanns was about 350, the population increased many thousands in the summer. In fact, there were so many people and so much traffic, every summer the village hired a policeman or two. The policemen used their own cars and attached a light to the roof to make the car an "official" police car. They mostly issued parking tickets.

One day, one of the policemen issued a speeding ticket based upon following a motorist. The ticketed person successfully challenged the ticket in court. The motorist's lawyer said the policeman couldn't prove his speedometer was accurate because it hadn't been recently calibrated.

The policeman went into great detail explaining to Dad, who was mayor at the time, why that wouldn't happen again. It involved something the policeman called "a fifth wheel." I never did understand what the fifth wheel was supposed to do.

Dad wasn't the least bit interested in matters concerning cars. He just nodded and said, "You're doing a fine job. I haven't heard of any major crimes in Fleischmanns recently."

Most of the summer visitors were Hungarian Jews who lived in or near New York City. They came to the mountains to escape the city's heat and humidity. Some stayed only a week or two. Others, especially retired folks, and young wives and their children, stayed for a month or for the whole summer. Working fathers would come up on the bus from the city late Friday afternoons and return on Sundays. There were many hotels and bungalows to accommodate them in and around town.

Many hotels, bungalow colonies, two or three grocery stores, a fish market, an antiquities store, a beauty parlor and a taxi service were among the businesses that opened up just for the summer season. They usually opened at the end of June and closed either right after Labor Day or after the Jewish holidays. The antiquities store was the most interesting place. It sold items from ancient times, like from the days of the Roman Empire.

The fish market was owned and operated by Charley and Sue Barrett, very good friends of my parents. Charley got his fish straight from the Fulton Fish Market in New York City. He (or one of his employees) met a truck in Kingston several days a week. I have seldom had fish as fresh as Charley's.

Whenever I went in the fish market, Charley always asked me some god-awful math question. He wanted me to do the problem in my head. He could, among other things, add columns of four-digit numbers and divide one three-digit number into another, all in his head. He knew one math shortcut after another, But he wouldn't explain his shortcuts. He'd smile when I asked him for a pencil and paper. "Oh, you shouldn't need that," he would say.

Sue, my mother, Grandma Mayes, and other ladies worked all year planning for and making things to sell at the annual Methodist Church bazaar. Grandma Mayes made aprons because, as she said, "That's all I know how to sew." She also made dozens of Parker House rolls. They sold out quickly. Mother made cookies, brownies, and cupcakes. Sue crocheted potholders, doilies, toilet paper covers, shawls, afghans, and other "fancy work" (as they called it). These things never interested me. The bazaar was the big fund-raiser for our church.

The church was on Main Street and the bazaar was held on the church lawn on a Wednesday in July. My mother left home early on the day of the bazaar and drove up to the church with the car loaded with things to sell. A few hours later, I rode my bike up to check things out. As far as I was concerned, the best part of the bazaar was Go Fish.

Mrs. Combs, a soft-spoken elderly lady who always had a smile on her face, always, well nearly always, ran the Go Fish. When the ladies set up the bazaar, they brought a brown-cloth-covered, three-panel folding screen up from the church basement and set it up on the right side of the lawn, near the baked goods table. A fishing pole with a safety pin for a hook leaned against the screen near Mrs. Combs. Mrs. Combs sat in behind the screen and there was a chair in front of it for each customer to sit on.

The customer gave Mrs. Combs ten cents and she handed the customer the fishing pole but kept hold of the safety pin. The customer then sat down. When Mrs. Combs said, "Go fish," the customer yanked on the pole. After a few yanks, Mrs. Combs let go and up popped a toy attached to the safety pin.

While not a big moneymaker for the church, it certainly provided the kids with something to do while their moms made the big purchases.

Brian, Dean, and I usually took some money for the bazaar from the small drinking glass that was nearly always full of change. The glass resided on the bottom shelf of the kitchen cupboard that held the drinking glasses. This glass system was Mother's invention.

Every once in a while, Mother or one of us kids would suggest that we get an allowance. Our allowances only lasted for two or three weeks because no one could remember to pay or to collect. The glass system met all of our needs and, amazingly, we were all trustworthy about asking for or reporting withdrawals. The church bazaar was an approved reason to withdraw change from the glass. No need to ask permission for that as long as the withdrawal was only a dollar.

Then there came the year that Mrs. Combs was ill at the time of the bazaar. What to do? Well, one of the frequent customers, who had now reached the advanced age of thirteen, said he would conduct the Go Fish enterprise. And an enterprising young man he was.

When the ladies counted up the money at the end of the day, the Go Fish coffers had about one-fifth the amount of money it usually had, even though the number of customers was about the same as in prior years. "Oh well. We learned our lesson," is all Mother said.

Once the bazaar was over, Mother would announce, "Well, now that that's over, I'm free. I really don't have anything on my schedule until it's time to get you kids ready for school." We never blocked out a week on the calendar for a family summer vacation. We all knew that Dad was too busy.

What happened in our family was that on a Thursday or Friday in late July or in August, Dad would get it into his head that the whole family should accompany him on a trip to Pennsylvania to see one or two of his customers. I think he really wanted a break from the mill and this was as good a way as any to get it. He would still be working, but not be at the mill.

Around ten in the morning, he would call Mother and say, "I need to go to Pennsylvania. Can you get everything packed so we can leave around twelve thirty? Also, we need some cash for the trip. Can you get it?"

Mother rounded up us kids, asked Grandma Mayes if she would feed the cat, and then packed the suitcases. Starting when I was twelve, she made out a check for five hundred dollars payable to the order of "cash" and gave it to me to take to the bank. I rode my bike up to the bank, presented the check to the teller (who was my father's cousin, the one with a wife who was "a horse's tail"), got the cash, and rode home. While I was a little nervous with all that money, I figured that no one would suspect a kid on a bicycle to have such a large amount of cash tucked in the pocket of her shorts. I felt so grown-up because Mother trusted me to do this big errand.

So, with all of the freedom my bike gave me, it also provided my parents with an opportunity to give me more responsibilities.

Chapter 8

Arguments with Mother

Me after a hated permanent, 1959

CAMP

While I liked school, I always looked forward to summer vacation. When I was in grade school, as the school year was drawing to a close, two important things happened. One, I subscribed to my favorite magazine, the *Weekly Reader*, and two, Mother invariably pulled out one or two sheets of paper and told me it was time to sign up for camp. I had a choice, Girl Scout camp or church camp. I had to go for at least one week, but she really wanted me to go for two.

Yuck.

"Why do I have to go to camp? We live in the mountains. Camp is for city kids. You know I hate camp. There is nothing fun to do there. I have so much to do here."

"Well, I just think it will be good for you. You need the experience of being away. We need to break these apron strings. It will be fun once you get there. Besides, it builds character. Which week do you want to go?" Mother always replied.

After days of arguing, some years, I would prevail. Other years, Mother would prevail and off I would go to camp.

Just as I'd predicted, there I was, sitting on some rocks in the shade, shivering, on the shore of some godforsaken lake. It was right after breakfast and I was waiting for my group's turn to go in the water, which was even colder than the air temperature. Utter craziness.

Then, when that torture was over, back to my cabin to change and get ready for lunch. Mmmm. Lukewarm grilled cheese, carrot sticks, and bug juice. Was it my turn to wash or dry the dishes after lunch? I could never remember. Oh well. Someone would tell me.

"Announcement. Announcement. Cabins one through four will play baseball on the big field today at three, and cabins five through ten will go to the crafts cabin to make pot holders," some counselor yelled as we were washing dishes.

Don't these people know anything about what sport to do when? I wondered. *Swimming in the morning and baseball in the heat of the afternoon. Where are they all from, anyway?*

I must remember to tell Mother that being around craziness doesn't build character.

Finally, as I neared the end of my high school career, Mother saw an article about a music camp at Hartwick College, my father's alma mater. Hartwick is a small liberal arts college in Oneonta, New York, a city about an hour from Fleischmanns.

"What do you think about going to a music camp this summer?" Mother asked one spring day. "It's at Hartwick College and you stay in a dorm room. It will be so much different than the other camps you have gone to and a good way to prepare you for college."

"Well, let me think about it. I have to agree that it sounds different than those do-nothing camps you have sent me to," I said.

"Here. Look over the literature. You take music lessons, which I'm sure you'll enjoy, and are in a chorus. Think about it."

A week later, Mother asked me, "Well, what do think about music camp? Do you want to go for three weeks or six?"

"I must admit, it does look better than those do-nothing camps. I'll sign up for three weeks," I said.

"I'm quite sure if you really like it, you can tell them and they'll let you stay for the whole six weeks," Mother said.

I loved music camp. Now here was a camp where I actually did things I wouldn't be doing at home. I took piano lessons, sang in the all-camp choir, and went to classes on things related to music.

At the end of my first week, Mother asked me if I thought I wanted to stay for the whole six weeks. I told her I didn't know yet.

"I think it would be a good idea for you to stay, especially if you're having a good time. But I just want you to know that I received a letter from Aunt Dort the

other day, and she, Uncle Ray, and Janet are coming
for a visit the fifth week you'd be at music camp, if you
decide to stay," she said.

"Thanks for letting me know. Are you having a
family reunion again this year?"

"Most likely. Everyone seems to like them."

I enjoyed our family reunions. Most of them
were held in our backyard. Nearly all of my relatives
from my mother's side of the family came; there was
always a lot of food, some beer (but this side of the
family weren't big drinkers), and lots of rounds of
croquet.

Grandma Cowan told me that her mother's
family had reunions. She and her siblings had them,
and now my mother, her sisters, and her one and only
cousin had them. We had them nearly every year,
when Aunt Dort, her husband, and her daughter came
east from Ohio.

On my mother's side, I had six first cousins, a
few great-aunts and great-uncles (only one of whom
had a child), and a few more-distant cousins. All but
Aunt Dort and her family lived within a morning's
drive of our house.

The more I thought about it, the more my
inclination was to go to the family reunion and not stay
at music camp for the whole six weeks. So I left music
camp after the third week.

My father's side of the family never had
reunions. In fact, his side was full of stories about
siblings not talking to each other for years over one
issue or another.

As children, Brian and Dean also went to camp,
Boy Scout camp. Brian actively liked camp and Dean
was neutral. When they were in their upper teens and
early twenties, they both took Outward Bound survival

courses. While both boys said these courses were tough, they agreed that they learned how to be resourceful and self-reliant.

In his three-day survival challenge, Brian caught a frog, killed it with his bare hands, and used it as bait. He caught a fish and ate quite well. His journal reflects that one of the things he missed the most was chocolate ice cream.

Dean took a winter Outward Bound course. In his three-day survival challenge, he was issued SPAM and rice, so food wasn't a problem. His water came from melting ice he chipped off the lake, and he heated his pup tent with a candle. (He had been issued a candle and matches.) His face and a few fingers suffered from mild frostbite, but he had no permanent damage.

My brothers' Outward Bound experiences were a far cry from the do-nothing camps Mother sent me to, that's for sure.

MY HAIR

Another one of Mother's quirks was that, for reasons I never figured out, every once in a while, she thought I should either get my hair cut short or have a permanent. I loved my braids. Each day, I absolutely loved deciding which of the six or seven colors of rubber bands I would use that day and whether to have two braids or one long "Chinaman's braid" in the back.

My friend Suzy gave me the rubber bands as a birthday present when I was eight. She apologized for forgetting to get me a "real" gift. This is one of two childhood birthday gifts from friends I still remember. The other one, also given to me by Suzy, was a blue-

and-white china cat. This cat now resides on the floor by my front door. Wow, is he old!

As school drew to a close, Mother would say to me, "Now that school is almost out, don't you think it would be nice to have short hair for the summer? It is so much easier to wash and take care of. I hear that Sally does a really nice job cutting hair."

Easier to wash, my foot, I thought. *Mother just pulls the ironing board up to the kitchen sink. Then I hop on and lie on my back with my neck on the edge of the board, head dangling toward the sink. Then, she pours pitchers of water over my head, adds a little Johnson's Baby Shampoo, rinses first with plain water, then with water with some vinegar (to get the last of the shampoo out) and finally with plain water. What difference does it make how long my hair is?*

No matter my reply, she would make an appointment and off we would go. I always made sure to slam the back door of the house as I made my way to the car and slam the car door after I climbed in the front seat. I complained the whole way to the hairdresser's, hoping Mother would turn around any minute.

Once at the hairdresser's, Mother explained what she wanted done and left. It didn't take long to ruin my hair if I had it cut. I'm sure I looked slightly better than I did at the age of four, when I'd cut off my bangs while standing in front of the tall mirror in the living room, but not much better.

Permanents were another story entirely. They took all morning, as in really all morning. *Who in the world would choose to sit in a chair for all of those hours with that horrid-smelling stuff on their head?* I wondered then and now.

After the deed was done, she picked me up, said how beautiful I looked, and added, "This will be so much easier to take care of. I'm sure you'll like it once you're used to it."

Once home, I ran to the tall mirror in the living room, took a look, and started to cry. I then ran to get my hairbrush and comb and tried to get my hair to look like it did before. This never worked. So I stomped my feet, threw my comb and brush, and spit on the rose-colored carpet.

"Mother, you know I didn't want anything done to my hair. I'm never letting you do this again!" I always said.

"It looks just fine. And it will grow out," was all Mother said.

"But I told you I didn't want to get my hair done. Can't you just leave me alone?" I always replied as I ran straight to my bedroom. I didn't go outside the rest of the day for fear of being laughed at.

Then, at dinner, Mother said, "Murray, don't you think Marilyn's hair looks nice?"

Dad always replied, "Why, I didn't even notice. Yes, it does."

What does he know, I thought. *He always agrees with her on stuff like this.*

Hoping to teach her a lesson, I didn't speak to my mother until the next afternoon.

I never understood her penchant for tinkering with my hair. To this day, I'm hesitant to go to someone new to "tinker" with my hair. I had one permanent when I was in my forties. Even then, I thought the whole thing took too long and smelled horrid.

Chapter 9

Counting Strips

One of the tennis rackets a manufacturer's
representative gave Dad, 1964

In May 1961, when I was eleven, Brian was
eight, and Dean was five, Dad said to us during supper
one Friday night, "Marilyn and Brian, do you want to
go to the mill tomorrow morning and count strips with
me?'

Brian and I looked at each other and Brian said,
"Okay. Do we still get paid a penny for each bundle of
twenty-five?"

"Yes. Just remind me to pay you when you're done," Dad said.

"Can I go this time?" Dean asked. "I want to go."

Because of his age, Dean was exempt from our earliest trips to the mill to work. But, as he grew older, it became clear to him that these trips to work at the mill weren't all work.

"Okay, " Mother said. "But you have to listen to Daddy and not run around down there. You know there are dangerous machines there."

"I know, I know. I promise to listen. Really," Dean said.

"Murray, you have to watch him like a hawk. You know how fast he is," Mother said.

"Yes, I know. I just think it's good for these kids to work a little. To learn what it's like to not have everything handed to them," Dad said as he took another helping of mashed potatoes.

"Well, I agree it won't hurt them," Mother said.

The next morning, around nine o'clock, Dad said, "Are you all ready? It's time to leave."

We all put on our jackets and piled into the car for the half-mile trip down Wagner Avenue to the mill. Usually we walked, or, should I say, Dad walked and Brian, Dean, and I ran to keep up.

Dad wasn't one for small talk. He was usually lost in thought, presumably about business issues. So our trips with him to and from the mill were silent, except for the chatter among the three of us.

Dad's mill made rotary-cut, hardwood veneer out of maple, oak, ash, birch, and cherry logs. He employed about 130 people, sometimes more, sometimes less, depending on how business was. He was one of the largest employers in the county and was under a lot of stress. Did he need to pay more for his logs so all the good logs didn't go to the sawmills? Which customers would he call to see if they needed more veneer? Why was the most recent truckload of veneer he'd sent to a customer in Pennsylvania so wet that the customer returned it? Could he afford to buy a second dryer? Did he have enough in the checking account to pay his employees?

The mill had three main buildings. One was used in production, and that is where most of the dangerous machinery was. The production building had a debarker, two lathes, big clippers that cut the long sheets of veneer into more manageable sizes, a dryer, and other equipment. A second building was mainly used to sort the veneer into various grades. A third building, which was attached to a three-room bungalow that served as the office, was used to cut some of the large sheets of veneer into smaller pieces. This is where we always counted strips for the princely sum of a penny per bundle.

One of our father's long-standing customers was a company that made tennis rackets. The company bent the veneer strips into the shape of a tennis racket. Several strips would be glued together to make one racket.

We followed Dad through the front door of the bungalow into the main office. I promptly plopped down in Helen's chair. Helen was a secretary, bookkeeper, office manager, and executive assistant all rolled into one. We learned early on not to touch things on Helen's desk. If we did, Helen would reprimand Dad, Dad would tell Mother, and Mother would scold us. Everyone was mad at someone. Not a good way to start the week.

As soon as Dad entered the building, he made a beeline for his desk, which was in a room next to the main office. He opened the bottom left-hand drawer and retrieved a Butterfinger, unwrapped it, and took a bite. He then started to look over a few pieces of paper on his desk, lost in thought while he turned his black mechanical pencil end over end, sliding his right thumb and index finger from the top to the bottom with each turn.

The three of us stayed in Helen's office. Soon, I was rolling around the office in Helen's chair and spinning in circles. Brian took the cover off The Machine. This was the one thing on Helen's desk we were allowed to touch. The Machine was very large. It was about eighteen inches wide, nine inches tall, and eighteen inches deep. It was one of the first calculators that did multiplication and division, a Marchant.

"Brian, let's see how much 10,234 plus 100,455 is," I said.

Brian said, "Oh, that's easy. We can always add, subtract, and multiply. Let's try dividing 367 by 121. Do you remember if we put the 367 in first or the 121?"

"I think it is the 121. Let's try it."

Brian tapped some keys, ending with the equals sign. The Machine fired up and started to churn away. It churned and churned. Dad was in his office, not paying any attention to us. Finally, I crawled under Helen's desk and unplugged The Machine, yet again.

"Guess that isn't it. Do you smell smoke?" I said.

"No. It's just your imagination," Brian said.

Meanwhile, Dean was over by the manual check-imprinting machine, inserting pieces of paper, pulling the handle down and producing fine works of numbered art.

Dad called from his office as he started to get out of his chair, "Time to get to work." He then bent over and opened the bottom left-hand drawer again. This time, he retrieved a 3 Musketeers bar. For a man who stood five nine and weighed 140 pounds soaking wet, he sure ate a lot of candy. "Ready?" he said.

We nodded and followed him out the back door into the attached building. I loved the smell of the room full of veneer. It reminded me of Dad, because this was how his clothes smelled when he came home from work.

Dad put on a pair of well-worn, leather, work gloves. He lifted a bunch of strips out of a cart and arranged them into three small piles on a table. The strips were sixty-four inches long, three and one-half inches wide and one-eighth inch thick.

"Here's a pile for each of you. Remember, twenty-five strips to a pile," he said.

"I can't reach," Dean said, with just his head showing over the table.

"Just try," Dad said.

Dean was on his tiptoes. "Eighteen, twenty, twenty-three, twenty-five," he said as he tried to make a nice pile of strips.

"Marilyn, will you recount Dean's pile for him?" Dad said.

"Okay. But then I get paid for it and he doesn't."

"We'll worry about that later," Dad said.

Dad took two of our piles of twenty-five and tied them together at each end with a special slipknot that his grandfather had taught him. He then placed the tied bundles onto the shipping pallet. When the pallet was full, black metal straps went around the whole thing. There was a red crimped clip that held the two ends of each metal strap together under tension. The pallets were shipped to customers by either railroad or truck.

Dad didn't put the metal straps on the pallet. He left that for someone more technically proficient than he to do on Monday morning.

After about fifteen minutes, Brian asked, "Dad, can we get a soda now?"

"Me too," Dean and I said at the same time.

Dad smirked and said, "After you each count four more piles."

After a few minutes, I said, "We're done."

Dad reached into his right rear pocket, pulled out his wallet with a small snap pocket for change, gave each of us a nickel, and told us to hurry back. We ran down a sidewalk, through the second building, down another sidewalk, and into the production building. We turned right and there, as always, was the beloved soda machine. We didn't have soda at home so this was a real treat.

The soda machine was a large red cooler without a lid. It was full of very cold water, and the eight-ounce glass soda bottles were held upright by the metal track they were in.

Brian put in his money and grabbed an orange soda. He moved it along its serpentine path to a gate that could now be opened. Dean also got an orange soda and I got grape.

As soon as we got our sodas, we pried them open using the bottle opener on the machine and took a sip. Then, Brian and I noticed the two battery-operated jacks that were plugged in to an outlet to be recharged. The jacks were used to move pallets of veneer.

The pallet jacks were orange. Each jack had two long, steel prongs on wheels sticking out the front that went under the veneer pallets. Usually the operator walked with the jack behind him, holding the handlebars that were connected to a long, steel column the operator swiveled left or right to steer the jack (like pulling a child's wagon). The operator needed to lower the handlebars at least fifteen degrees from its spring-loaded upright park position to disengage the electric brake and safety stop. The machine made a loud click when the handle passed the "go" point, indicating that the electric brake was off. The operator then twisted the handles one way to make the jack go forward and the other way to make it go in reverse. The greater the twist, the faster the jack would go. To stop the jack, the operator either reversed the twist on the grip to return the grip to the neutral position and let the jack gradually come to a stop, or raised the handlebar to an upright position, which automatically cut the power and applied the electric brakes.

When we first started operating the jacks, we stood on the forks in the back (where the pallet would normally go), leaned very far forward, pushed the handlebar down, and twisted the handles just a little bit because we weren't comfortable going fast. Then, as we became more proficient, we sat on the massive battery compartment with our legs hanging over the front of the jack and increased our speeds dramatically. Sometimes we went around corners so fast, the edges of the jack scraped the floor and we feared it would tip over. It's difficult to believe that Dean was only five when he started taking the jacks out for a spin, especially once you realize the jacks weighed over half a ton and could reach speeds that were equal to a very fast walk.

As soon as we saw the jacks, we put our sodas down on the concrete floor, unplugged the jacks, and each hopped on one.

"Beat you to the dryer," Brian said to me.

"No you won't."

"Wait for me!" Dean said as he ran behind trying to catch up.

And so began another day at the races on Wagner Avenue.

When we didn't return to our assigned duties, Dad came to look for us. "What are you kids up to?" he said. "Put those jacks back and be sure to plug them in."

"I got only one ride," Dean said.

"You'll have more chances next time," Dad said as he strode back to the building where the strips were.

When we returned to the building where Dad was, there was a large push broom leaning up against the table. "Here, Dean. Why don't you use this to sweep the sidewalk between this building and the next one? Come get me when you're done."

"Okay," Dean said as he grabbed the handle and pushed the broom out the door toward the sidewalk. Dad smiled upon observing that the broom was taller than Dean.

Dean returned in about twenty minutes and shouted from the doorway, "Dad, I'm done."

Dad, looking over the job, said, "Not too bad for the first time." And, motioning to a section with a lot of dried mud, he said, "Just do this area again."

When Dean finished, Dad said it was time to go home for lunch. He gave Dean a quarter for sweeping the sidewalk and Brian and I each got fifty cents for our morning's work.

"We want a raise. This isn't enough for all of our work. How much do you pay your regular workers?" I said.

"This is about all of the profit I make on these. I can't afford to pay you any more."

Several years later, when Brian was twelve and needed some excitement after a morning of counting strips, Brian said to Dad, "Can I have the car keys? I want to take the car for a spin."

"Me too," I said. "I want to drive first. I'm the oldest."

Dad reached into his left back pocket and pulled out his car keys. He gave them to Brian. "Be careful. After you drive a little, give Marilyn a turn. Dean, you're too young. But it won't be long 'til you're big enough. Don't be too long. We have to go home soon."

The three of us ran out to the Lincoln Continental. Brian moved the electric seat up as far as it could go and made it as high as it could go. I was in the front passenger seat and Dean sat in the back. Brian started the engine, turned on the radio, changed the station to one with rock 'n' roll, and off we went for a drive around the mill yard. The ride was very bumpy because the yard was full of rocks and huge potholes.

Soon, whenever we went to count strips, we asked Dad to drive us to the mill so we could all practice driving after a hard morning's work. One fateful day, when Brian was fourteen, he took the car for a drive around the mill yard after a week of steady rain. The mud in the mill yard was deep, and the next thing he knew, he was stuck. He put the car in drive and then in reverse to try to rock it free. No luck. He got out and got Dad. When Dad saw how deep the mud was, he shook his head and said, "I'll have Percy get the Huff and tow it out tomorrow morning." Percy was in charge of the log yard and knew how to operate the big equipment there. Our father didn't even know how to start the Huff, much less how to operate it.

For years after that incident, when Percy came to work on Monday mornings, he said to Dad, "Murray, have any cars you need towed today?"

Then there was the Saturday that Dad's work ethic seriously clouded his judgment, at least in Brian's and my opinion. (Dean wasn't at the mill that day.) Brian, Dad, and I were counting strips, and around noontime I said, "Dad, I'm hungry. Can we go home for lunch now?"

"No, we have to finish this cart," Dad said, pointing to a cart half full of strips that needed to be counted and tied into bundles.

About fifteen minutes later, Brian said, "Dad, I'm hungry too. Can't we go home for lunch?"

"No, we're still not finished. I have to get this order out tomorrow and we aren't done."

We asked Dad to let us go home for lunch every fifteen minutes or so for the next two hours. As we got more and more hungry, we started to cry, but Dad just ignored us. Dad didn't get hungry like regular people. He just got a headache. And he was in a mood to teach us what hard work was like.

Finally, by two o'clock we were done and Dad said, "I guess we can go home for lunch now." By this time, Brian and I were very hungry and very mad at him. We walked home, both of us in tears.

When we arrived home, we told Mother that Dad hadn't given us lunch and we were starved. Mother said in her sternest voice, "Murray, you can't work these kids that hard. They're too young." It didn't happen again.

The result of all of our hard work of counting strips became apparent one day when Dad came home from the mill with two strung tennis rackets. A representative of Dad's customer had visited the mill that day and given Dad the rackets so he could see exactly how the veneer was being used. I always suspected that in the numerous conversations Dad had with the representative, Dad used the famous and usually effective "indirect method" to obtain the rackets.

The indirect method is a subtle, or not so subtle, way of getting a person to do a particular thing through dropping hints that are sufficiently obscure that the person does what you want while thinking the whole idea of doing the thing was his or hers.

So, I suspect Dad mentioned to the tennis racket manufacturer's representative that he had children and lived across the street from two wonderfully maintained tennis courts. If the message didn't get through the first time, Dad would simply try various versions of the indirect method over and over. When a person finally caught on to what Dad wanted, Dad would grin. Obviously, the representative got the message.

We were elated! We had never used the tennis courts and didn't have a clue as to the rules of tennis.

Our first order of business was to go up to Gale's Store and buy tennis balls. Mother gave us money because, Lord knows, our wages from counting strips wouldn't cover such a purchase.

Brian, Dean, and I took turns using the rackets and, at first, just volleyed back and forth. Finally there came a day when we decided we were ready to learn the rules.

We didn't know anyone who played tennis, but the *Encyclopedia Britannica* came to our rescue once again.

There, in the encyclopedia, were the rules with a diagram of the court. The article explained which lines were for singles play and which were for doubles. We read the rules several times and consulted with Mother about the meaning of many of the sentences. But, after asking her a few questions, it became apparent she knew even less about tennis than we did.

So, armed with a few of the rules, we went across the street with our tennis balls and rackets to the courts to play. When some of the tourists arrived, we realized quickly that our interpretation of the rules wasn't totally accurate. But if we went over to the courts when they were full and sat quietly on a bench, we soon learned most of the rules by simply watching and listening to the other players.

During the spring and fall, it was easy to get a court. But, since Fleischmanns was a summer resort town, we often had to wait for a court in the summer. We usually just looked out a living room window to see if there was an empty court before going over. But, sometimes, we would think a group was getting ready to leave and we sat on a bench by the courts to wait.

At least once a month, while we were waiting for a court, one of the tourists would say to us, "You know, you should wear white on the court."

Our usual reply was, "Yup, we know." And, then one of us would say in a loud whisper (hoping to be overheard), "Where do they think they are, Wimbledon?"

It was clear the summer tourists wished we would simply disappear. But, since we lived in town year-round, we didn't let this attitude bother us. We knew they would be going home to the hot, old city any day and the courts would be ours again.

The most helpful instruction we ever received from a tourist was from a man in his thirties. We were just finishing up and he was coming over to take possession of our court. He said to me, "Do you want a helpful hint?"

I said, "Sure. Can you wait a minute until my brother gets here?" Brian was on the other side of the court and I motioned to him to come over.

As soon as Brian arrived, the man said, "Here's what you do."

He then rolled a tennis ball that was on the court to the outside of his right foot, pinched the ball between his foot and the racket, and raised the ball up off the ground by lifting his leg straight up. He let the ball go, it bounced off of the court, he hit it straight down with his racket so it would bounce higher, and then he caught the ball with his left hand.

That was it! That was the big lesson. What a disappointment.

To this day, whenever I play tennis, I smile as I occasionally pick up the ball using the no-bending-over method and think about earning a penny a bundle.

Chapter 10

Trees, Houses, and Carpentry

Tree house with tennis courts and Palace Hotel
in background, 1965

THE SECRET ROOM

Except for riding our bikes, jumping on our pogo
sticks, roller-skating on the sidewalk, or sitting on
lawn chairs singing Christmas carols at the top of our
lungs in July, we spent very little time in the front
yard. Unless, of course, you consider the hours we
spent climbing the pine tree. Starting at the age of
eight, I frequently climbed higher than the house, up to
where the trunk of the tree was only four or five inches
in diameter. A few times, I had to ask Brian or Dean to
get Mother because I couldn't figure out how to get
down. She would come out of the house, look up, and

calmly tell me to put my left foot on the branch that was just below the one it was on, and then put my right foot on a branch that was part way around the tree, but lower, and so on until I was in familiar territory. She never yelled at us for going so high.

One fall day, when I was eleven and my cousin Danny was twelve, we were a good three stories up in the tree. Danny pointed to the attic and said, "Where's that window? I don't remember seeing that in the attic."

"I've no idea," I said.

So, off we went to the attic. As far as we knew, the attic had three main rooms and a crawl space over the middle room. The crawl space was the only secret place we knew about.

After searching all around the attic for an hour or so and going up and down the tree to confirm our sighting, we discovered a real secret room. We could access it only by crawling on our hands and knees through a narrow space against the eaves of the front room of the attic. Once we made our way through the short, narrow passageway, we peered into a room with a steeply gabled roof to the left and the right and a small window straight ahead. The room had only floor joists with white fluffy insulation between them.

"Aha. That's the window we could see from the tree," Danny said while pointing to the very small window with, strangely, a rotten, yellow, sheer curtain barely hanging in it.

At dinner when we told Dad about this discovery, he said, "I know about that room." Then I realized, of course he did. Not only had he lived in the house most of his life, he, his sister, and his parents had lived in the attic while renting out the rest of the house in the summers during the Great Depression.

"You have to be careful up there. If you step on the insulation, you will come through the ceiling in Grandma Cowan's room," Dad said.

"Can we put a floor in? Danny wants to," I said.

"Yes, but just be very careful," Mother said.

We found some plywood in the basement and, with Danny as the engineer, added the floor. Installing the floor took several days. We started by laying the plywood at the entryway. Then, we laid the plywood down the middle of the room and finally out toward the eaves.

"Oh no—I slipped into the insulation and I think I heard a cracking sound," Brian said.

"Not again! Marilyn, can you go down and look at the ceiling in the bedroom to see if there is a crack?" Danny said.

In a few minutes I returned and reported that all was well.

As we progressed toward the eaves, there soon came a point where there was simply not enough space between the eaves and the joists to raise a hammer to pound the nails into the plywood. As far as we were concerned, the floor was finished.

We never spent a lot of time in this secret room because even with our heads directly under the peak, we couldn't stand up straight. In addition, the attic was very hot in the summer and very cold in the winter. So the room was habitable only in the spring and fall.

This is the first carpentry project I remember Danny being in charge of. He must have inherited some of the Mayes carpentry genes that had totally skipped my father.

THE TREE HOUSE

"Mom, will you take Danny and me to Wadler's for some lumber? We want to build a tree house," Brian asked late one morning at the end of July 1964 when he was twelve and Danny was fifteen.

"Let me talk to your father when he comes home for lunch. Where do you plan to put the tree house?"

Mother always ran important matters like this by Dad. Otherwise, Mother was totally in charge. Well, at least she was in charge of Brian and me. Dean was another story.

When Brian saw Dad walking home from the mill, he ran to meet him. He told him of Danny's plan to build a tree house. With a sheepish grin, Dad said, "I hope you can get it finished before he moves to Florida. I'm certainly not going to finish it for you. You know that my grandfather's and great-grandfather's carpentry gene skipped me."

"Hey, we know. You've told us a thousand times," Brian said.

By now, we kids knew that while Dad could barely pound a nail, his great-grandfather Harrison (Hat) Mayes had built the Palace Hotel, which was next door to the tennis courts, and his grandfather Howard Mayes had built many houses in town, including Ruth Carey's, some stores and hotels, and the theater on Main Street.

We also knew that while our father could run a business and, by using something we called The Mayes We, he could get others to work for him.

"The grass is getting pretty high. I think it's time we mowed the lawn," Dad said on more than one occasion to Brian or Dean.

We were well into our teens before we started to call him on using both The Mayes We and the indirect method.

"Dad, can't you just plain ask us to do something?" one of us often said to him. "Just what part of this 'we' includes you?"

He would give a small chuckle followed by a sheepish grin and say, "Well, my method usually works, doesn't it?"

Of course, we all had to agree that it took us years to catch on. And it took even more years to conclude he was incurable. Even when he was in his eighties and in a nursing home with dementia, he was still getting the nurses to do things for him by using The Mayes We and the indirect method. And most of them seemed happy to please him. That's the way it always was with my dad.

"Just where do you plan to put this tree house?" Dad asked as he continued up the walk.

"In one of maple trees by the front sidewalk. Danny has it all figured out," Brian said.

Danny was moving to Florida in the middle of August, so he would be there in time to start eleventh grade. We were all confident that if we worked really hard we could finish the tree house before he left. At the time, Fleischmanns High School had three geniuses, and Danny was one of them.

After lunch, I called Danny and gave him the good news—we had permission to build the tree house. Now he just had to finish up the plans so we could go get the lumber, nails, and bolts.

The next morning, Danny rode his bike the half-mile up Wagner Avenue to our house with his plans. Soon, he, Brian, and Mother were at Wadler's lumberyard loading lumber into the trunk of the car.

After several trips, they had everything they thought they needed.

Brian and Danny worked long and hard, and they finished the tree house two days before Danny moved. Dean and I were carpenter's helpers. Our main tasks were handing up a piece of lumber or picking up dropped nails and hammers.

The tree house was magnificent. It had a roof, and the spaces between the boards that made the sides were wide enough to serve as windows. We had a good view of the street below. An important feature, to be sure. It was twelve feet off the ground, and entry was achieved by climbing a rope ladder that we pulled up once inside. A critical design element.

We soon realized that just sitting up in the tree house was boring. It wasn't a good place for smoking. Mom would smell the smoke when she sat on the front porch. Besides, we already had a great clubhouse for smoking.

The first few days, we ate lunch in the tree house. But that soon became passé. One night at dinner we were bemoaning our lack of ideas of what to do in the tree house when Dad said, "Why don't you tie a string around an old wallet and yank it up as someone bends over to get it?"

Brian then suggested we use almost invisible nylon fishing line instead. So, the next morning, Brian rode his bike up to Gale's Store and bought the line.

Mother found an old wallet into which we inserted a dollar bill with the edge sticking out. I tied the fishing line around the wallet and off we went to the tree house. As soon as we climbed in, we pulled up the ladder.

We dropped the wallet out of the tree house to the sidewalk immediately below us. We sat there, trying to be very quiet as we saw our first customers walking down the street. It was a Jewish couple in their seventies who were out for a morning stroll. The lady was the same one Brian and I had intentionally brushed up against the preceding night on Main Street. She had been wearing a mink stole. We loved walking around town brushing up against the soft fur stoles with our bare arms. We always followed these encounters with a very quick, "Oh, excuse me."

We always had on our shorts and short-sleeved shirts when we went for our evening walks to rub against the furs. We were never cold and never understood why so many ladies came to the mountains with their furs. We knew it was cooler in the mountains than in the city, but seriously. Some of the stoles had an animal with its head biting its tail. Yuck.

The lady was now in a short-sleeved dress, and she had Nazi concentration camp numbers tattooed on her left forearm. Mother had explained to me what the numbers meant. The cruelty these numbers represent is something I just couldn't, and still can't, comprehend.

The woman saw the wallet first. Speaking in German, Hungarian, or Yiddish (we never knew which), she pointed to the wallet. As her husband bent over to pick it up, Brian yanked on the line and the wallet flew into the air.

The man jumped back and yelled something, which of course we didn't understand. He and his wife looked up, saw the tree house, and began to laugh. In English, he said, "Very good. Very funny. Very funny." We, of course, were bending over with laughter.

The trick worked even better in the early evening, as it was starting to get dark. Often my whole family except for the person in the tree house was sitting on the front porch in the wicker furniture. The furniture was still very sturdy even though it had been Grandma Mayes's living room furniture when Dad was young.

Dad would sit in the straight chair reading the paper for as long as he had enough light to see. Mom would sit in the rocking chair and two kids would sit on the sofa. Mom and the kids would be chattering away. We all had our feet resting beside the citronella candles that were on the cobbler's bench that served as a coffee table. Mother's father had used the bench to repair his family's shoes and his horses' harnesses.

"Got another one," Mother said as she swatted yet another mosquito that had landed on her arm.

"I guess these citronella candles help a little, but the mosquitoes still bite me," she said as she pulled a tissue out of her apron pocket to pat the small amount of blood that the dead, smushed mosquito left on her arm.

"Look, here come some customers," Brian said as another elderly couple approached.

Everyone stopped talking and Dad put the newspaper he was reading down in his lap. We all wanted to see if someone would bend over to pick up the wallet. Some potential customers just kept on walking. What a disappointment.

Of the customers who went for the wallet, nearly all of them located our tree house without a problem. We soon realized we needed to make some improvements.

Brian came up with the idea of tossing the line over the power lines and tree branches to the sidewalk on the other side of the street, the side next to the ballpark. It didn't take us long to find a smooth and clear path. We also realized that it was always best to have just one person in the tree house. Silence was very important. Besides, the rest of us were more comfortable and had a great view of the action from the front porch.

Our first customers on the ballpark side were a young Hasidic couple with two small children. They always walked in the following order: husband, wife, and, finally, children. I always felt sorry for the Hasidic children because, in my opinion, they had on too many clothes for summer and looked hot. As the husband went for the wallet, Brian pulled it up. The husband spent a good two minutes trying to figure it all out. His wife laughed, but he didn't find the situation very amusing. At last he pointed to the tree house and shook his finger at it, saying, "Not funny. Not very funny."

We did the wallet trick every two or three weeks on the theory that the people who had seen the trick would have checked out of the local hotels and a new group would have arrived. This proved to be accurate.

The next summer, we set up our trick and as a group of adults approached it, one of the men held out his hand to stop another man from bending over for the wallet. He was grinning and, pointing to the tree house, said, "Look up there. It's a trick. I remember." Then, Dean, who was manning the tree house, yanked the wallet to demonstrate and everyone laughed.

Once Dean realized the trick was becoming well known, he knew he needed to do something else. So, with Brian's help, they got out the six-foot stepladder and tied several pinecones to the maple tree. Then Dean just sat in the tree house waiting to see if anyone noticed.

Soon a man and his six-year-old son came walking down the street. The son, pointing up, said, "Dad, can you get me a pinecone?" The father picked up a stick and tried to knock the pinecones off the maple tree, but had no success. The father shook his head and said, "Guess they're not ripe."

Too bad Danny missed most of these adventures in the tree house. It certainly provided us with hours of entertainment.

Chapter 11

Fall Meant Fires

Pinewood Hotel one day after one of its many
fires, early 1960s

When summer rolled to an end, the tourists left
for New York City, the hotels and bungalows closed for
the season, and school started. There were always a
few former hotel employees, nearly always men, who
stayed behind. We sometimes saw two or three men
bundled up in their heavy coats, rocking away in the
sun on one or more hotel porches even though the hotel
had closed for the season. They had dragged a few
rocking chairs out of wherever they had been stored
and were smoking away while enjoying the fall air.
When we drove by one of these hotels in the evening,
there were seldom any lights on because the owners of

the hotel had the electric power turned off. At most, we might see a light in one of the downstairs hotel rooms from a flashlight or lantern.

As the nights grew colder, some of these "bums" (as Mother called them) left town. Often, Mother received reports from some of her friends when one of the bums finally boarded a Trailways bus to the city. But often, before all of the bums left town, the inevitable happened. There would be a fire at some hotel or another.

The fires were nearly always at night. Someone would drive by a hotel, see flames, go home or to the nearest establishment that was open (that is, a bar), and pick up the phone. The operator would say, "Number, please."

The person would say, "I would like to report a fire. There is a fire at XYZ Hotel."

I would be sound asleep and the fire sirens would go off. There was a siren at the firehouse, which was located at the upper end of Main Street, and a siren right across from our house, near the tennis courts. They always rang seven times. That was the signal to the volunteer firemen who were at home to pick up their phone and ask the operator where the fire was. The operators knew who the volunteer firemen were and which lights on the switchboard belonged to them. So the operators would take their calls first. After learning where the fire was, the firemen drove to the firehouse, got either one or two fire trucks, depending on the anticipated severity of the fire, and drove to the fire.

Before leaving the firehouse, one of the firemen would write the location of the fire on a chalkboard at the firehouse. This enabled firemen who heard the siren but who weren't near a phone to easily find out where the fire was if the trucks had already left.

The hotels were all large wooden structures and went up in flames in a flash. The fires were huge. The main job of the firemen was to keep the fire from spreading to the trees or to neighboring buildings. Usually they were able to put out the fire before the whole structure was consumed. In retrospect, all this achieved was leaving a place for yet another fire next year. Sometimes the firemen called for mutual aid, and fire companies from neighboring towns would come to help fight the fire or go to the Fleischmanns firehouse and stand ready to respond to another call if, God forbid, one came in.

Fires were quite a social event. In fact, sometimes one or more of the firemen brought out a bottle of liquor to ward off the cold of the evening. You saw people you hadn't seen since the last fire. There was always a lot of gossip about how the fires started and whether the electricity had been turned off. Had anyone seen any bums living there recently? Had the hotel had a good season or were the owners nearly bankrupt and possibly looking to collect on their fire insurance?

The Takanassee Hotel fire was especially huge because it was one of the largest hotels in the area. After the fire had been raging for an hour or two, Mother looked at her watch and said, "Dean, it's later than I thought. We must get home. You have to get to bed because you have a Regents Exam tomorrow. You won't do well if you're tired."

"Can't I stay just a while longer? I really did study."

"Okay. Just five more minutes. You know there will be other chances to see big fires," was the way Mother summed up her decision and the reason for it.

Even Dean had to admit Mother was right. This wasn't a once-in-a-lifetime event.

If the fire siren went off and Dad was home, there was a sense of panic. Mother immediately went to the phone and asked the operator where the fire was. While she was waiting for the operator to get to her call, Dad would either be walking quickly down to the mill or, if he had been asleep, he would be dressing in a great hurry. Sometimes he was a quarter of the way down to the mill before Mother went out to the front porch shouting, "Murray. Murray. It isn't the mill!"

I remember the fire being at the mill only once. One night, the man tending the wood-fired boiler went to sleep and the fire got out of control. Fortunately, there wasn't a lot of damage. When I asked Dad what happened to the man, he said, "What do you think happened? I fired him."

That made perfect sense to me. The man nearly caused the whole place to burn down.

I was in high school when I learned that Dad had very little fire insurance on the mill. When I asked him why, he said, "All of my profits would go to fire insurance premiums. I'd have no money left over for anything."

Is it any wonder that for years I got a knot in my stomach every time I heard a fire siren?

When I went to college, I was surprised to learn that very few people had seen huge fires. They were so common when I grew up that I thought everyone witnessed them.

Fall brought more pleasant fires; the ones everyone in those days set to burn leaves. What a wonderful smell! The rules against polluting the atmosphere by burning leaves hadn't been enacted. In fact, as far as I know, no one even thought about the issue.

We loved to burn leaves. First, we raked the leaves that were on the front lawn into huge piles and jumped into them. Then, when we tired of that, we raked them into the gutter. If there wasn't much wind and the leaves were relatively dry, we got permission from Mother to ignite them. We were each assigned a section of the long row of leaves to ignite and to monitor. It usually took a few matches to accomplish our goal, or at least we acted like it took a few matches.

We then stood guard, rakes in hand. Our job was to keep the fire contained to the gutter. Most cars slowed down as they passed the burning pile. They didn't want to blow the burning leaves all over the road, thus blocking it. Occasionally a car would drive by much too fast and we had to rake the errant burning leaves from the middle of the road or from the yard back to the gutter. This was a little exciting because you had to accomplish the task before the next car came or leaves on the lawn caught fire. What a responsibility.

Raking and burning leaves occupied us for several weeks at the end of October and the beginning of November.

While we were raking leaves, Mother invariably asked us, "What do you kids want to be for Halloween?"

Brian and Dean often had ideas, while I seldom did. I never really liked Halloween. I have never liked asking people for money or anything else, including candy at Halloween. Give me nearly any other task to do and there is a good chance I'll do it gladly. Just don't ask me to solicit people for money or anything else. I must have been born this way.

To make Halloween even more trying for me, neither Mother nor I was very creative when it came to making costumes. She tried, but it certainly wasn't one of her strong points. One year, my cousin Danny was Santa Claus and I was a clown. Another year, Danny was the White Rabbit and I was Alice in Wonderland. He pulled me in his little red wagon. I must say, I was a terrific Alice with my blue eyes and long blonde braids. Mother even had Mrs. Hubbell make me a powder-blue dress that I wore for as many years as Mrs. Hubbell could make it fit.

Two of the worst costumes Mother made were for Brian and me. We were cigarettes. I was eleven and Brian was eight. In retrospect, she should have completed the theme and made Dean a costume as a match, but she didn't think of this. Clearly this was long before the U.S. Surgeon General's report on the dangers of smoking. The costumes were made out of cardboard.

Well, they did look like cigarettes. I'll give her that. Over a period of two or three weeks, Mother had us stand very still so we could try on our costumes as she constructed them. They came down to our knees and fit perfectly. There were holes for our arms and eyes, but she forgot one thing. We couldn't walk in them.

Each Halloween, the local Rotary club sponsored a parade around the high school gym where, when the parade was over, the judges awarded prizes in various categories. If you were selected, you were taken out of the parade and stood on the stage so you could be awarded your prize. I think the prizes were cash. But, having received only one or two, I really have no memory of what the prizes were.

Well, the year we were cigarettes, the first challenge was getting in the car for the ride to the school. We had to take off the costumes and put them in the trunk. Once at the school, we had to stand ever so still while Mother dropped the costumes over our heads and aligned the holes in the cardboard to our eyes so we could see where we were going.

"Okay, you're ready now," Mother said.

Off we went to join the parade. The first obstacle was the set of five steps we had to descend to get to the gym. Mother held on to the cardboard as I rather toppled down the steps. Once I was down, she helped Brian down. Then we went through the door to the gym to join the parade.

There was no way we could keep up. We were taking baby, or more accurately, infant steps. We kept falling down and others in the parade had to help us up. Sometimes there was a minor pileup. Once we were on our feet again, the holes in the cardboard didn't align with our eyes. The people who helped us up didn't think about that. So I just looked down at my feet and shuffled along, bumping into things and falling down again and again. Whose idea was this, anyway?

Eventually the judges selected Brian and me. I was so happy because I finally had a costume that merited a prize. We were on the stage at last. Still as two statues.

The next day Mother said, "I'm sure they awarded you kids a prize last night more out of concern for the safety of others and sympathy than because they thought your costumes were so good."

What a letdown that statement was! Here I'd thought we had really good costumes.

The other prizes the Rotary awarded the night of the parade were for the best-painted windows in town. Drawing! Another skill set I totally lack.

In mid-October, most kids would try to find another kid or two who might be interested in painting a store window. The school had a list of ten or so merchants on Main Street who were willing to have their windows painted. Each team then had to have the store owner sign a permission slip that you took back to the school secretary, June. She then gave you a complete set of the authorized bottles of water-based window paint. Each set had eight colors: black, white, green, orange, yellow, red, blue, and purple.

We had about ten days to complete our paintings. If I was lucky, my partner (usually my friend Pam) had some ideas for a picture and the ability to draw. That would leave me to provide moral support, hand over the right bottle of paint when requested, and paint the large areas that my partner had outlined. I could handle this level of responsibility.

Usually our pictures had some variation on the theme of green grass, several orange pumpkins, a black fence, a white moon, a black cat, a black witch on a broom, and/or a black crow. We would paint a little, and then walk up and down Main Street to see what the competition was doing. Some kids waited until the last minute to paint because they didn't want anyone to steal their ideas. Some of the scenes were amazingly good.

So even if you didn't participate in the Halloween parade, if you or some of your friends painted a window, you came to the school on Halloween to see whose windows received a prize.

I don't think any of the windows I helped paint ever received a prize.

The rules of the window-painting contest required us to wash and dry the window we had painted until it was up to the merchant's standards. That is, it had to be sparkling clean. Depending on what day Halloween fell on, we sometimes had only five days to accomplish this. And, of course, the weather always took a turn for the worse immediately after Halloween.

I swear, it could have been sixty degrees on Halloween; and if it was a year I painted a window, as soon as Halloween was over, the daytime highs were in the low forties. If you were lucky, the store had running hot water to fill your buckets with and the merchant let you use his squeegee. The worst thing was washing windows with cold water on a cold day. It was on these days that I would make a mental note not to sign up for window-painting next year.

As the days grew shorter and it got colder, there would come a day when Mother announced at dinner, "When I was in the post office this morning, I overheard Jimmy say that no one has seen anyone on the porch of the Pinewood Hotel for about a week. So, I guess all of the bums have left town. They just have no idea how cold it gets here in the winter. They're much better off in the city, anyway."

Chapter 12

Thanksgiving and Christmas

Me, 1953

Thanksgiving was (and remains) one of my favorite holidays. I liked seeing the stores decorated for Thanksgiving and I liked the story of the first Thanksgiving. I also liked the fact that everyone celebrated it, no matter your religion. No remembering to say, "Happy Holiday" instead of "Merry Christmas."

I liked Thanksgiving Day because it was as relaxing as a Sunday but I didn't have to get up to go to church. And there was none of the stress of being prepared for school concerts or church pageants.

Even though Dad didn't like turkey, we had the typical Thanksgiving dinner: turkey, stuffing, mashed potatoes, salad, cranberry sauce, gravy, Hubbard squash, two other vegetables, and dessert. To please

Dad, Mother usually also had scalloped oysters. I still haven't developed a tolerance for even the smell of them, though all reports were that Mother's were very good.

Dad loaded his plate with the oysters and took one small piece of turkey, which Mother always carved in the kitchen before we sat down to eat. Dad was as good with a carving knife as he was with a hammer.

We ate Thanksgiving dinner in the dining room, used the good silver with the everyday dishes. We seldom had any company for Thanksgiving. It was just the six of us, counting Grandma Cowan.

After Dad said grace, Mother invariably said, "That was very nice, Murray. Thank you. I know turkey isn't your favorite, but it's just not Thanksgiving without it."

Then there would be a big discussion as to whether to pass the food to the left or to the right. In the end, we all agreed that it didn't matter, just as long as all of the food went in the same direction.

As Mother and I were clearing the table after dinner, Mother always said, "That tasted good. Murray, the kids and I will eat the leftovers. I won't even subject you to turkey soup."

"I guess it was all right. As long as we don't turn around and have it again for Christmas," Dad always replied.

Grandma Cowan and I washed and dried the silverware and Mother put away the leftovers. After Grandma and I were done with the silverware, Mother put the dirty dishes in the portable dishwasher that she then hooked up to the kitchen faucet.

In a few weeks, Christmas activities started. It was a busy season. For several years, I accompanied the school senior choir on the piano and played the flute in the band. Brian played the trombone and sang in the choir. Dean sang in the choir but, after trying the French horn for a few years, drew the line at playing an instrument. Mother didn't fight this battle very hard.

We were also in the church Christmas pageants. The big difference between these and the school concerts is that these involved learning (or, more likely, reading) a few lines about the religious significance of Christmas and a little acting. I usually accompanied the children on either the piano or organ, depending on what the occasion called for.

"Mother, Pam and Cathy asked me to go to bowling with them on Saturday. But I have to practice the solo piano part in one of the senior choir pieces and the concert is next week, finish reading my book and do a book report, finish my math homework, go to Sunday school, and then play the organ at church. I just don't know if I have the time. And then there is that crazy church pageant next week that I have to play for," I said one Friday night at dinner.

"It's hell to be popular," Grandma Cowan said in her ever-helpful tone.

"Well, I'm sure you have time to go bowling if you practice the piano and do your math homework after dinner," Mother said.

"Okay. I'll call them and let them know that I'll go with them."

Brian and I never complained about being in the church pageants. If that is what Mother said we were supposed to do, we did it. Dean, on the other hand, was never interested in being in any of the church pageants and he made his thoughts known.

Dean's best friend Mel (whose grandfather was related to Grandma Mayes) was of the same mind.

Every year, Mother and Mel's mother tried every tactic in the book to convince them they had to be in the pageant. The mothers always won, but it was always a battle.

It isn't that Dean was unfamiliar with the church; he just had another view of what one did there. Starting around the age of eleven, he spent most of his free time in the church basement with one of the pastor's sons and other friends. They smoked, listened to the radio, and played poker. Dean continually lost all of his money to his older friend Stuart. Stuart had been playing poker for years with the guests of his parent's hotel. Dean never had a chance against an experienced player like Stuart.

At Christmastime, my parents gave gifts to the customers of the mill. Some years, the customers received large boxes of chocolate candy. Of course, there were always a few extra boxes for us. The boxes were stacked in tall columns in the front entryway to our house because it was cool there. Other years, the customers received large marquetry pictures.

In both cases, Mother spent hours wrapping the gifts on our dining room table, first in seasonal paper and then in cut-up brown paper bags so she could label them for mailing. This took her hours.

"Don't bump into the table. You know I'm trying to write," Mother would firmly say to Brian as he sat down in a dining room chair after school while setting a heaping dish of chocolate ice cream on the table.

Our parents also gave the employees of the mill boxes of food at Christmas time. Mother gave a lot of thought as to what to put in the boxes. Every box had a frozen turkey, fresh squash, potatoes, canned cranberry sauce, ingredients to make a salad, and some canned pumpkin to make pie. She tried to make sure the people with the largest families received the largest turkeys.

Finally, it was Christmas Eve.

When I was five, at my father's suggestion, I left four Lorna Doone cookies and a glass of milk for Santa to help him on his busiest of nights. I carefully set them out on a plate and included a paper napkin, just in case he needed it.

Very early the next morning, I got my parents up and we headed downstairs. "Look Dad. He ate every cookie and drank all of the milk. He sure must have been hungry," I said. "Do you see how messy he is? There are crumbs everywhere." Clearly this wasn't my image of Santa. But at least he enjoyed what I had left him.

"It's a good thing you left him something," Mother said.

After surveying the scene, I went straight under the tree to retrieve my presents. The presents Santa brought weren't wrapped up. Only the gifts from our parents were.

We always opened our presents on Christmas morning. We received a few toys and games and quite a few clothes. We really needed the clothes because while Mother would buy each of us a few new things when school started, we were starting to run low on clothes that fit. Interesting how Santa knew exactly what we wanted (or needed) and in the right size, no less.

We had Christmas dinner in the early afternoon. Christmas dinner was always beef, usually prime rib and mashed potatoes. Dad always complimented Mother on the meal and added, "I'm so glad we aren't having turkey."

When Christmas was over, there was still a week to go before school started. If we were lucky, it was cold enough for ice-skating and there was enough snow for skiing. But we would go skiing only a few times because the lift lines were long. As a result, we spent many hours in the house doing crafts and whatever else we could think of.

When we were young, one of our chief activities was wrestling each other on the dining room floor, right beside Grandma Cowan. Grandma Cowan spent most of her day in a rocking chair by the large dining room window reading a book, the newspaper or *TIME* magazine, or knitting mittens.

Not only was wrestling great entertainment, but also we knew it bothered her. If Mother was out doing an errand, Grandma Cowan thought she was in charge.

"You kids are going to kill each other. Stop it right now. Do I have to get my cane after you?" she yelled.

"Grandma, we are only play-fighting. Mom lets us do this all the time," Brian replied.

"Stop it right now, I say. Stop it!" she said as she got up out of her rocking chair and went for her cane.

Upon seeing her go for her cane, we would stop wrestling and run to the other side of the dining room table. She would come after us and the merry chase around the table was on, Grandma running after us waving her cane and yelling.

Soon Grandma would tire, sit down in her rocker, and wipe her brow.

"You kids are awful, just awful," she said.

"We know, we know," Dean said.

When Mother got home, we would tell her what had happened and she just said, "Can't you kids behave for even five minutes while I'm gone?"

Another of our favorite activities was watching Grandma Cowan watch TV. One of her favorite shows was *Studio Wrestling*. Yes, the same person who reprimanded us for wrestling watched it on TV.

"He's cheating. Look at him hold that guy's leg!" she shouted as she sat on the edge of her chair about four feet from the television. "That's right, you go get 'im," she said while shaking her fist at the screen.

"Grandma. That's so fake," I said on numerous occasions.

"Well, he still shouldn't be doing it," Grandma replied.

Another favorite show was *Queen for a Day*. In this show, three women told the audience what horrid situations they were in. A typical situation would be a wife with twelve children who was married to a very sick and out-of-work husband. All she really wanted in life was a washing machine.

After hearing the stories, the master of ceremonies held his hand over each woman's head and asked the audience to vote on who should have her wish granted. The audience voted by applauding and the show's "applause-o-meter" measured the volume. The people at home got to see the needle on the applause-o-meter climb for each woman. After the final vote, the woman with the highest reading on the applause-o-meter was crowned and robed as the Queen for a Day. The curtain parted and there would be a new washing machine and a case of detergent.

The Queen for a Day always wept and Grandma Cowan said, while she wiped her eyes, "She really deserves to win. She has such a hard life. I don't know how she does it."

I was always glad when Christmas vacation was over and it was time to go back to school and to return to my normal routine.

Chapter 13

Winter: The Beginning, the Middle, and Will It Ever End

Dean, Brian, and Me ready to go skiing, 1966

Winter in Fleischmanns could begin at Thanksgiving and last until mid-April; or, it could begin after New Year's and be over in early March. You just never knew. Most years, there was a January thaw and then a week in February when it was twenty to twenty-four degrees below zero when we got up to go to school.

One day in February 1962, I was having my breakfast of apple pie and a cup of coffee with milk and three teaspoons of sugar when Mother said, "It's quite cold this morning. Twenty-two below right now, and the radio said it probably won't go much above zero today. So I'll take pity on you kids and drive you to school, provided the car starts. Marilyn, when you are done eating, call Linda and Richard to see if they want me to pick them up."

We usually walked the three-quarters of a mile to school, but when it was very cold or raining cats and dogs, Mother would take us.

As soon as I finished eating, I went to the dining room and picked up the black desk phone. A woman's voice said, "Number, please."

I said, "Three, four, six," and soon heard Lucille, Linda and Richard's mother, say, "Hello."

"Hi, Lucille. It's Marilyn. Mother is going to drive us to school today and we can pick up Linda and Richard in about ten minutes."

Lucille was a very modern mom. She always insisted we call her by her first name.

"Very good. But if your car doesn't start, I'll drive," Lucille said.

"Okay. I'll tell Mother."

The three of us plus Mother bundled up and piled into our car, which was parked in our driveway. Mother pumped the gas pedal several times and then turned the key. The next thing we heard was the car churning and churning. After quite a few churns, a cylinder or two fired, and then the engine died. Soon, the battery started to fade and Mother said, "Well, I guess the car isn't going to start until it warms up a little. Go on over to Lucille's, her old Buick always starts."

Brian, Dean, and I trudged through the fifteen inches of snow in the Towels' backyard to Linda and Richard's. I knocked on the back door. Lucille came to the door with her hair in curlers. She had on her slippers and her long, partially buttoned bathrobe that, more or less, covered her long, sheer nightgown. Her lack of carefully applied makeup made her look much older than usual.

"Come on in. I guess your car didn't start," she said. "Linda. Richard. Put on your coats. Time to go. I'm driving." Lucille then put her bare feet into her calf-length fur-lined boots, slipped on her mink coat, and turned up the collar. She tied a silk scarf quickly around her curlers, found the car keys in her pocketbook, and put on her ski gloves.

"Let's go. I'm ready," she said.

We all piled into her car, three in the front and three in the back. Nice and cozy for such a cold day. Lucille was one of the first wives in town to have her own car. It was a used 1952 four-door, dark-green Buick sedan. It was a wonder. Everyone loved it.

She pumped the gas pedal a few times, turned the key, and the car fired up. We were off.

"Don't you just love this car?" Lucille said as she turned around looking at us while the car wandered into the middle of the road. But, since very few cars would start, there was no real danger of being hit. We all agreed that it was the best car ever made.

Of course, we nearly always walked home from school, unless it was pouring or didn't get much above zero all day. When we were very young, Mother picked us up in the school parking lot on those days. Once we were old enough to walk home on Main Street, she picked us up where the alley that started in the schoolyard terminated on Main Street.

The alley had its own social life. I was never part of it. It was the place where kids started to smoke or made out. They all huddled behind a chimney so they couldn't be seen from the street. It was also an excellent place to light matches since the chimney blocked the wind. Only those of us walking across the bridge from the schoolyard to Main Street knew who was there and what they were up to.

I had no desire to smoke. I had been smoking cigarettes, string, and corn silk at home for years. What was the point of standing there, anyway? I had better things to do than to stand around with those academic underachievers. And why would anyone start this expensive habit? *Oh well, each to his own,* I thought.

Hooray! Mother was there. As I got into the car, she said, "It sure is cold. It never got above zero today. It's supposed to warm up tomorrow and a big storm is forecast for Thursday night."

"Maybe they'll cancel school on Friday," I said.

Our school never closed because it was cold. It only closed if we had an ice storm or a big snowstorm, a big storm being defined as one where we got over twelve inches of snow in a short amount of time. If the snow fell during the night, we would listen to the radio in the morning to see if our school was closed.

We listened to WGY, a fifty-thousand-watt radio station broadcasting from Schenectady. It was the most reliable station we received and it had all the school closings. Bill Edwardsen, the host of the morning show, would read them. Since they were in no particular order, you had to stay glued to the station until you heard your school's name announced. Fleischmanns High School was never one or two hours late, like some schools. We were either open or closed.

If there was no school, we literally jumped for joy. We had so many decisions to make. When we were in grade school, after breakfast we put on our snowsuits and headed out to test the snow. If it was packable, we made snowmen and igloos.

Snowmen required a trip or two inside to get carrots for the nose and sometimes an old scarf or hat. Occasionally we had whole snowmen families: a mom, a dad, and two or three children. Our neighbor Ruth Carey had a furnace that burned coal. So when she came home from work, we asked her for some coal for each snowman's eyes and mouth.

Igloos were only possible when the piles of snow on either side of the front steps were very tall. We collected the flour and sugar scoops from the kitchen and the small hand gardening tools from the icehouse in the backyard. Digging to hollow out the snow piles was tough because we had to be on our backs for a lot of it. We felt like coal miners. One or two of us were diggers and the others hauled the snow out of the way and patched holes in the roof. Often, Linda and Richard helped us.

"I'm going in the house to get a bowl of water," Brian said. "We need to turn the snow into ice."

Soon all five of us were traipsing in and out of the house with metal bowls and measuring cups of water to splash onto the walls and ceiling of the igloos.

After one or two trips, someone suggested adding food coloring to the water. I made a quick search of the cupboard where the baking ingredients were located and produced small bottles of yellow, green, red, and blue coloring. We never used yellow, for obvious reasons.

But, try as we might, we just didn't have a good way to throw the water up onto the walls and ceilings of the igloos. Our mittens and snowsuits were soon wet and then we got very cold.

On a few occasions, school was canceled because of an ice storm. Two of the ice storms were so terrific that, in the morning before the sanders reached

Wagner Avenue, we put on our ice skates and skated in the road all the way down to the mill and back. "So this is what it's like in Holland!" we remarked to each other.

When I was in high school, we perfected making ice cream. Frequently, Mother, who loved sweets, said to us, "I'm going up-street in a few minutes for the mail and a few groceries. Do you kids want to make ice cream this afternoon? If so, I need to get more milk, cream, and eggs, and maybe some rock salt."

Brian and I always wanted to make chocolate and Dean always wanted vanilla. If Mother was busy, she settled the dispute by deciding we would make chocolate chip. If she wasn't too busy, we would make both chocolate and vanilla.

Soon after Mother returned with the mail and groceries, it was time for lunch. We could see Dad walking up the street coming home from the mill. He had a quick, short stride. He loved a hot lunch, especially in the winter. Mother usually had his favorite lunch: homemade soup with warm saltines and strong cheddar cheese cut from a huge wheel at Bussy's grocery store.

During lunch on a snow day, Mother frequently reported, "It's a good thing I didn't need bread today. Solomon's was almost out of bread. Dave told me the bread truck couldn't make it over Pine Hill this morning. He's quite sure he'll get some in tomorrow."

Dad said, "The storm was a little worse than I realized. Some of the workers didn't make it in today."

During all of this winter activity, Grandma Cowan occasionally said, "Do any of you need new mittens? I feel like knitting this afternoon. Marilyn, if you'd like, I'll teach you how to knit and purl the German way. It's such a better way."

"I need new mittens," Dean said.

"Bertha, do you have some odds and ends of yarn? I always like to make striped cuffs."

Then, Grandma Cowan went up to her bedroom to get her five double-pointed knitting needles. When she returned, she made a beeline to her rocking chair that was beside the large dining room window. I never understood why she made such a deal about where her cane was. If she had a mission, she never seemed to need it, in spite of her claim that she was always dizzy.

I sat on the floor beside her, hoping that she didn't smell too bad today. For reasons that I never understood and much to Mother's consternation, she never took a bath or shower. And, most shocking of all, she used a chamber pot at night even though her bedroom was right next to the upstairs bathroom.

It's not as if Mother didn't try to get her to take a bath or shower. I heard them argue over it many times. It's just that Grandma Cowan refused, even when Mother offered to help her in and out of the tub.

"I wash up in the sink. That's good enough," Grandma said.

In fact, her penchant for not bathing led to another one of our entertainments. Sometimes, while she was sitting on the edge of the dining room chair watching TV, we would take it up on ourselves to improve the smell around her. One of us would go into the tiny downstairs bathroom and retrieve the can of squirt air freshener that always resided on the tank of the toilet. When we returned to the dining room, we took turns squirting it all around her.

"What are you doing?" Grandma said to us, turning around in her chair. "What's so funny?"

"Oh, nothing," Brian said, hiding the air freshener behind his back.

I thought she probably wouldn't smell too bad today because she had recently returned from her yearly stay in the hospital. Once every winter, Grandma Cowan would be admitted to Margaretville Hospital for a few days because she had a cold.

Whenever this happened, I asked Mother, "Is Grandma Cowan really sick?"

Mother always replied with a little chuckle, "Not really. This is just her yearly vacation. She likes to take hers in the hospital."

How weird, is all I ever thought. *But Mother must be right. She doesn't act very concerned and she is a nurse.*

Today, the smell wasn't at all bad and I really did want to learn how to knit.

"Go ask your mother for a set of big regular knitting needles and some fat yarn. I will show you how to knit and you can knit a cat blanket. After you learn that, I'll show you how to purl," Grandma Cowan said.

When I returned with the supplies, she cast on the stitches and showed me how to knit. I was struggling with my stitches. Some had fallen off the needles and the few that remained were very tight.

"Look Gram, this is a mess. I'll never get this," I said.

"Don't worry. All new knitters knit tight. You'll get it," she said.

Grandma Cowan was the oldest of four children. She, her younger sisters Bertha and Emma and their parents Albert and Amelia Ploutz Koutz came to America in 1890 or so from Germany. Her mother was pregnant with Julius when they were at sea. Grandma's memories of the crossing were of how sad and seasick her mother was.

They were on the ocean at Christmastime. Grandma Cowan always remembered her mother spinning wool fleece into yarn on the spinning wheel they had with them. As her mother spun the yarn, she sang "Silent Night" in German with tears streaming down her face.

As Grandma Cowan, age six, was getting off the ship with her family in New York City, a well-dressed man got off a fine carriage that was drawn by two beautiful brown horses and approached her father.

"Can I buy your daughter? You see, my wife can't have any children and she so wants some," the man said, tipping his head toward the well-dressed lady in the carriage. "We will give your daughter a wonderful home and everything she wants. She has such beautiful blonde hair and blue eyes. She looks so healthy. She's just what we are looking for."

"No thank you," Grandma Cowan's father replied. He then explained that he and his family had relatives in Roxbury, New York, and they were going to the Catskill Mountains.

Albert found work in Lexington, New York, and the family lived there for a year or so. He was paid a dollar a day and received room and board for his family. After setting aside enough money to buy (or make a down payment on) a farm, he bought a dairy farm in Roxbury, where Grandma Cowan's sister Bertha, her brother, Julius, and his wife still lived. The farm was only a few miles from the Cowan farm in New Kingston. They were on opposite sides of the same mountain.

I never asked Grandma Cowan whether the conversation with the stranger was in the German dialectic they spoke, High German, or English. Grandma Cowan knew her father spoke High German because she had heard him converse with a man in High German once when they were on a train in Germany. She didn't understand much of the conversation and was very impressed with her father. He told her he had learned it in school and she too would learn it when she went to school.

Grandma Cowan started school after she arrived in Roxbury. She didn't know any English, but she soon learned it in school. The family spoke as much English as possible at home because they were now in America. Grandma Cowan told me her parents realized that to get ahead in America, they would have to become as fluent as possible in English. As a result, whenever I asked Grandma Cowan to speak to me in German, she could count to one hundred and say a few more things, but that was all.

"You know, we were very poor when I was a child," she said. "I had to stop going to school when I was fourteen and go out to work. I lived with a family on their farm and helped the wife in the house."

I couldn't fathom living away from home at such a young age.

"The people were nice to me, except that I had to work all of the time. Even in the evenings. If I wanted to sit in the parlor by the fire in the winter instead of being in my cold, dark bedroom, I had to be knitting socks or mittens. I could never just sit there and rest. That was hard," Grandma Cowan said.

As I continued to struggle with my cat blanket, Brian ran into the kitchen and said, "Mom, can we make the ice cream now?"

"We'll start it right after I take a quick nap. You know how I get if I don't get my nap," Mother said. "You kids can grate up the chocolate for the chocolate chips and get out the ice cream maker. It's in the fruit cellar. Brian, will you test the motor and soak the wooden bucket in some warm water in the laundry room sink? We need to swell up the wooden slats."

When Mother got up from her nap, she cooked up the custard sauce that, when put into an ice cream maker, turns into ice cream. She poured the sauce into the metal container with the dasher in it. The dasher is a paddle that churns the custard sauce as it freezes into ice cream. She then placed the metal container into the wooden bucket and attached the motor to the top of the container. Brian took everything out to the back porch.

Brian was in charge of the ice cream maker from soup to nuts. Dean and I were mere helpers. As Dean and I filled the wooden bucket with snow, Brian added just the right amount of rock salt and hot water from a teakettle. The result was a cold slurry that, because of the salt, was colder than thirty-two degrees. As Dean and I made trip after trip to get more snow, Brian sat on a step pushing the new snow into the bottom of the wooden barrel with a wooden spoon in one hand and slowly adding hot water with the other. Occasionally, he would stop and scoop in more rock salt. After a while, he had the slurry just as he wanted it, and his job then was to listen for the motor to change pitch, an indication that we now had ice cream.

Plain vanilla and chocolate ice cream were relatively easy; chocolate chip was another story. If we added the chips too soon, they would melt and we ended up with weak chocolate. If we added them too late, the dasher couldn't mix them in. After a couple of years of experience, Brian mastered the art of making chocolate chip ice cream.

Our homemade ice cream always tasted a little like rock salt because the hole where the dasher emerged from the container so it could attach to the motor wasn't properly sealed. I loved this salty taste. Apparently, everyone else did too since the ice cream seldom lasted past our bedtime snack.

It was common on snow days for the sun to come out around noontime and for the afternoon to be beautiful and sunny with temperatures in the mid-twenties. A perfect day for skiing, but who would take us to Belleayre Ski Center?

Sometimes the phone rang soon after breakfast and it was Linda. "Want to go skiing? Mom is going to try to make it up to Belleayre."

Belleayre Ski Center is owned and operated by New York State and is twenty minutes from Fleischmanns. Lucille was one of the few adults in town who skied. She learned as an adult and loved it. Our mother thought she was crazy to ski.

"How is the family going to manage if Lucille breaks her leg?" Mother said, as she proceeded to worry not only about her own family, but everyone else's, too.

"Sure. We'd love to go skiing," I said to Linda.

We put on our ski clothes and lace-up ski boots, got our skis and poles, and went over to Linda and Richard's. We put the equipment in Lucille's dark-green Buick and off we went.

On one of these trips, Lucille had no trouble on the main roads because the plows and sanders had been out. But the road to Belleayre had only been plowed. There was no sand in sight. We had very little trouble getting up the lower half of the mountain road to Belleayre, but once the road got steep, the old Buick's tires started to spin and the car fishtailed back and forth.

"I can make it," Lucille said as she backed the car down the hill, put it in drive, hit the gas, and let her rip.

We made it a little farther, but still had quite a ways to go. She repeated the process several times. We burned rubber as we went. The car fishtailed all over the road and filled with the smell of burning tires. After about the fifteenth attempt, she finally gave up. We were so disappointed. We knew there would be no lift lines that day.

Then, of course, there were the times it snowed and school wasn't canceled. I would look out of the school windows and wish we could go to school on Saturday and ski during the week when there were no crowds.

During the first week of January 1967, I was complaining about the fact that I had to go to school when the skiing was so good. I was a senior in high school and thought it might be a long time before I would be able to ski in such wonderful conditions so close to where I lived. I had been talking to one of my best friends and classmate, Steve, about this sad state of affairs. He told me his mother had given him permission to skip school on these days during his senior year. It was a reward for the excellent scholastic work he had done.

When I got home from school I said, "Mother, Steve's mother is going to allow him to skip school when the skiing is really good. Can I skip, too?"

"Let me talk to your father," she said.

That evening, after dinner, Mother came to me and said, "Daddy and I agree that you can skip school and go skiing when the skiing is really good. But I'm not going to lie about your excuse. I'm going to say exactly what you did. If there are any problems, it'll be up to you to handle them."

"Okay, no problem. Thanks, Mom," I said.

Steve and I skipped school five or six times that winter and had a wonderful time. We often made fifteen runs in a day because there were so few people skiing. We usually went down one of the beginner slopes for the first run and used the rope tow or the T-bar. I always liked the rope tow and T-bar because if someone had trouble getting on or off or there was an equipment failure, I could easily ski back down the hill.

After our inaugural run, we took the chairlift to the intermediate and expert slopes. While the chairlift took us to the more challenging trails, I never liked it when the chairlift stopped as I sat there high off the ground. I wasn't particularly afraid of heights, I just didn't like sitting still while the wind blew all my body heat away. I usually got off in the middle of the mountain so I could ski the intermediate trails down to the lodge. Steve, who was a better skier than I, usually got off with me. But sometimes he went on up to the expert section. When he did that, I would ski slowly so he could catch up to me.

Occasionally we would both go up to the expert section. He would guide me down. He was always very patient, waiting at various points to make sure I made it safely down a particularly steep part. I would traverse across the mountain and make a stem Christie turn. Of course, I would fall, but the safety strap connecting each ski to my bootlaces prevented my skies from careening down the mountain. Steve usually made parallel turns. After I had fallen a few times, I would simply give up for a while and just sideslip down the steepest parts. Steve would encourage me to traverse and do my stem Christies the whole time.

Neither of us was ever called into the principal's office or reprimanded for skipping school even though our excuses clearly stated we had gone skiing. For what it's worth, I was first in my class of sixteen and Steve was second. Steve died in his early thirties. There is no doubt; skipping school was the right thing to do.

Chapter 14

Making Maple Syrup

Fireplace, patio, and Dean, 1961

I never thought I would be vindicated. But during my first year of college, Mother said I had been right all along. This is how it happened.

In many places, late February and March are thought of as early spring. In Fleischmanns, these months are often just a continuation of winter, only a little warmer. Some of the largest snowstorms of the year often come in March.

When the daytime temperatures reached the mid to high thirties and it was still below freezing at night, we knew it was time to make maple syrup. This was quite the production, but we were up to it.

At the beginning of syrup season, Brian and Dean would go to the cellar to get the brace and bit, the one-and-a-half-gallon tin sap buckets, and the spiles. Dad had identified which trees in our yard were hard maples, suitable for tapping. The first year, Mother helped us decide where to drill the holes, taught us how to insert the spiles, and hang the buckets. Even Grandma Cowan was excited. She loved syrup time.

Making maple syrup takes a lot of patience because it is common to have to boil down forty gallons of sap to make just one gallon of syrup. So, as you can imagine, a lot of our efforts were spent in trying to figure out how to improve the evaporation process.

Some days, especially at the beginning of the season, the sap would really flow. We would empty the buckets into a large container before going to school and, amazingly, the buckets would often be overflowing when we got home. The sap didn't flow quite as fast at night, but there was usually quite a bit of sap in them each morning. Some days, there was a block of ice on top of the buckets that we would scoop out and throw on the ground. We thought this resulted in a little less water to evaporate.

Frequently, on his way to school, Dean stopped at one of the buckets, filled one of Dad's old metal Kodachrome film canisters with sap, and screwed on the cap. He then stopped occasionally as he strolled to school to take a sip. The sap was usually gone by the time he reached school and, since Dean is left-handed, the canister was safely stored in his left jacket pocket.

When we first started to make maple syrup, we boiled down the sap on the electric stove in the house. After about two days of this, Mother said, "You kids have to do this outside on the fireplace. I just can't have the kitchen walls and ceiling coated with maple sap steam. You're making a mess of my stove and, besides, it's difficult to get supper when you have two burners of sap going. There is an old pot in the fruit cellar you can use."

I went to the basement for the pot and the charcoal. Brian and Dean got newspaper and matches to start the fire in the outdoor fireplace. This worked well the first year when we had only a few sap buckets out.

By the second year, we were really in the spirit. We got more equipment and put three or four buckets on each of our four maple trees. When we looked at the supply of charcoal left over from the previous summer, we realized we would run out. Since it wasn't traditional cookout season, the local stores didn't have any charcoal in stock. Charcoal wouldn't appear in the stores until Memorial Day. But we had a source of wonderful, free wood: scraps of veneer from the mill.

"Mom, will you take us down to the mill so we can fill up the trunk with veneer?" I said one afternoon.

"Sure. Just let me call your father to let him know what we want," Mother said.

So we three kids and Mother went to the mill and filled the trunk with scraps of veneer. The trunk was so full, the car bottomed out several times as we drove out of the pothole-filled mill yard.

"Guess we shouldn't have gotten quite so much veneer. We'll know better, next time," Mother said.

When we got home, Brian, Dean, and I stacked the veneer as best we could in neat piles beside the fireplace. We then covered it with a plastic sheet to keep it dry.

What a fire the veneer made! It had been through a dryer at the mill and most of it was maple that was a quarter-inch thick, three or four inches wide, and about a foot long. It burned like a charm.

At supper, after the first day of burning the veneer, we reported to Dad that his veneer made the best fire imaginable. Now our only problem was that we needed pans that had more surface area, so we could evaporate the sap faster.

In a few days, Dad brought us two pans. He had asked Frank, the man who fixed anything and everything at the mill, to build us some sap pans. The pans fit exactly on the fireplace grates and were four inches high. They were wonderful. Now we were in business!

About the fifth day, when we were in full production mode, I went up to my bedroom to get a sweater. The chimney to the fireplace was against the outside of the house right by my bedroom. I heard a dull roar. I felt the wall and it was very warm. I ran downstairs and asked Mother to come up. When she felt the wall, she said, "I think we have a small chimney fire. Let's get the hose out."

When we got back to the fireplace, Mother said, "Brian, go down cellar and get the hose. We have a small chimney fire. Squirt the hose on the side of the chimney, right by the house."

"Mother, don't you think we should call the fire department?" I said.

"No, we can't do that. Those men are busy working. We can handle this," Mother said. She didn't want to bother the men who served in the Fleischmanns Volunteer Fire Department, if she could help it.

While Brian went to get the hose, Mother carefully moved the two sap pans to the far end of the picnic table so none of the water from the hose would get in them. She didn't want to set back our syrup making any more than necessary.

Mother hooked up the hose and then made sure one of us kids stayed outside to squirt water on the chimney until the fire was out. During dinner, Brian, Dean, and I took turns manning the hose. I ran up to my bedroom every half hour or so. I put my ear on the wall where the chimney was and felt the wall to see if it had cooled down much. After two or three hours, the fire was out but my room smelled of smoke.

This happened every year when we made syrup. I have no idea why we kept using the fireplace. The scenario was the same each year.

I usually had a difficult time sleeping after these fires because my room smelled of smoke and I thought the fire would start up again. When I complained to Mother, she said, "Oh Marilyn, just relax. I'm sure the fire is out." My brothers also thought I was just being my usual nervous self. No sympathy from any quarter.

We usually finished the maple syrup inside. Grandma Cowan taught us the last step. We put just a drop or two of milk into the syrup. All of the wood ash and other debris in the syrup collected around the milk and was easy to scoop out.

Often, we boiled some of our syrup to the soft-ball stage. Then, we would go out and get bowls of clean snow and drizzle the thick syrup over it to make lockjaw. It's a great-tasting candy and fun to eat. Once you eat it, you'll know how it got its name. When we had our fill of lockjaw, we simply stirred the leftover thick syrup, poured it into a greased pan, and had maple candy.

Then there came the year when the roar in the chimney was louder than usual and my bedroom wall was warmer than usual. We got the hose out but we ust couldn't seem to quell the fire. Finally even Mother was a little scared. So what did she do? Did she finally call the fire department? No. They were all too busy. She called Dad.

Dad came home with two men from the mill. One of them had hands with huge calluses. As soon as he arrived, he went to move one of the metal evaporating pans off the fireplace grate. He knew the value of maple syrup. As he reached for the very hot pan full of boiling sap, Mother asked him if he wanted a pot holder. He said with a smile, "No, I'm fine."

They got the fire out, and Mother and Dad both concluded that this was the end of our maple syrup making. The next day, I asked Dad if the man had burns on his hands. My father was sure he didn't.

In 1968, our parents had a lot of work done on the back of the house, including having the fireplace and its chimney removed. To everyone's amazement, the chimney had no lining and was simply a three-sided brick structure with the clapboard siding of the house as the fourth side. Not surprisingly, the siding was severely burned. Who would ever dream a chimney would be built this way?

When I came home from college soon after this remodeling project had begun, Mother said to me, "Marilyn, you were right. Those were real chimney fires. The house really could have burned down. I should have listened to you."

Chapter 15

Spring Vacations

Me (in Grandma Cowan's rocker) with a view of
a corner of dining room table, living room and carpeted
stairs, 1957

For reasons I never understood, when I was in
elementary and high school, schools had a two-week
vacation in early April. It was called "spring vacation."
What a misnomer. The first two or three days were
fine. We had some projects to do and played a few
games of Careers, Flinch (a card game using cards with
just the numbers 1 through 15), Monopoly (using our
father's childhood board), and Carrom (using our
mother's great-uncle's board). I was the best at
Careers; it was a draw when it came to Flinch and
Monopoly, and Brian was by far the best at Carrom. In
fact, Brian is excellent at anything that requires hand–

eye coordination. Carrom is a great game. It is like pocket billiards played on a wooden board that is about thirty inches by thirty inches. Since Brian was by far the best player, he now has the board and the playing pieces. One sad fact about the board is that the varnish is missing in one large spot on the back side because our yellow cat (one of our favorite cats) peed on the board once when he was sick.

After playing these games for a few days, boredom set in. Nearly all of the snow had melted, so there was no skiing, and it was too cold and windy outside to ride bikes or roller-skate for long. No one's family in our school took a big spring vacation. All the parents just kept on doing whatever they did when we were in school. The concept of going away in the spring hadn't yet arrived, at least in the Catskill Mountains. But occasionally, our family went to New York City for the weekend during spring vacation.

Our parents loved opera, so we often went to the Metropolitan Opera. I usually enjoyed it, but Brian and Dean hated it. Dad took us to the Metropolitan Museum of Art and to the Museum of Modern Art. Mother didn't enjoy museums the way Dad did, so she sometimes did something else. Dad often took us to Grand Central Station to look at the ceiling with its lighted stars. I always marveled at how busy the place was.

Both of my parents knew their way around the city. After World War II was over, Mother's tour of duty as an army nurse ended and she lived in Manhattan for two years. She worked at Columbia Presbyterian Hospital and studied for her B.A. in nursing. Dad spent quite a bit of time in New York when he worked for a co-op store in Weehawken, New Jersey, after receiving a B.S. in chemistry from

Hartwick College. Dad might have stayed in Weehawken longer, but his parents had asked him to come home after his father was diagnosed with prostate cancer. The family needed Dad to help run the new family venture, a veneer mill.

When we went to New York City, we sometimes stayed at The Statler Hilton. Soon after we arrived in our room, a bellman would deliver a basket full of fruit. This always puzzled me. No other hotel or motel that we ever stayed in did this. Mother loved fruit and was usually pleased with the selection.

One time while we were at this hotel, there were many people from the press and a lot of excitement in the front of the hotel and in the lobby. My parents asked a few people what was going on, and we learned that Fidel Castro would be coming through the lobby in a few minutes. He had just finished making a speech at the United Nations. We went to the mezzanine where we could look down to the lobby. No sooner had we stationed ourselves in the front of the mezzanine than Fidel Castro strode through the lobby to the elevators. He wore what I thought was a strange outfit to make an important speech in: army fatigues. He had a beard and was walking purposefully while waving at the crowd. He was well protected by his bodyguards.

When I asked Mother why he was so important, she explained that the current ruler of Cuba was a dictator and that Castro wanted to bring freedom to the people of Cuba. However, she explained that there was a division of opinion in the United States as to what he would actually do if he came to power.

One of the biggest thrills of my life was going to see *My Fair Lady* on Broadway with my mother. I loved every minute of the show and couldn't believe how lucky I was. I was in seventh grade. I loved the costumes, the story, and the music. Very few children in my class went anywhere, except maybe to Kingston, which was forty-five minutes from Fleischmanns, or saw anything in the way of theater other than school plays and the movies. I thought about this as I enjoyed every minute of the show.

I also loved going into the large department stores: Lord & Taylor, B. Altman, Saks Fifth Avenue, Macy's, and Gimbels. I remember standing in the vestibule of Lord & Taylor on Fifth Avenue with my mother one day about fifteen minutes before the store was to open and being served hot tea in china cups with saucers. How refined. I felt so grown-up surrounded by ladies holding china cups that were tinkling and the smell of hot tea everywhere.

A contrast to the elegance of having tea in the vestibule of Lord & Taylor was having lunch or dinner at an Automat.

"Let's have lunch at the Automat," Mother often said. "They're quick and I think it is something the kids should experience."

"They're quick, I'll give you that. But the food is nothing to write home about," Dad replied.

What a weird place, I thought. *Putting all of that food in a glass-enclosed case. Mother's right—it's different, all right!* I would peer through the glass doors at the selections of sandwiches, select one, put some coins in the slot by the door, and then open it to retrieve my sandwich. There was nothing like this in Fleischmanns, or anywhere else I'd been. It certainly was an adventure to come to New York City.

Sometimes we went to the rodeo or the circus at Madison Square Garden. How could all of those clowns fit in that tiny car? The trapeze artists were superb.

One year, I even saw my heroes, Roy Rogers and Dale Evans.

While some of our cab rides were thrilling, we always pestered Dad to take us on the subway. After buying tokens (coins the size of dimes with a hole in them in the shape of a "Y"), he put them in the slot on a turnstile so each of us could get inside the station. Dad always knew whether we wanted to go Uptown or Downtown. Once on the right platform, he paid attention to the number or letter of each train as it came to a stop, often letting one or two go by because they weren't the right train. This led us to believe he knew what he was doing.

Eventually one would come along and he would tell us to hop on. As soon as we were on the subway, he made a beeline for the map and studied it to ascertain where the train was really going. I never understood why he did this after we boarded the train. Often, just as the doors were closing, he quickly stood up and said, "Let's get out of here. Hurry."

More than once, he said, "I've made a mistake. We are on an express train. This isn't going to such a great neighborhood. We're going to get off at the next station, go up the stairs, and catch the next train downtown. Just follow me. You'll be okay." And we were.

We usually returned from New York on Sunday afternoon after going to Radio City Music Hall in the morning. Mother always said that was a great way to spend Sunday morning, unless we were going to go to church. Radio City was a real treat. There was always a full-length movie followed by the Rockettes. No matter what time of year it was, the Rockettes were always performing.

When we got back from New York, we still had a whole week of vacation left with nothing to do and nothing to look forward to. When I was in elementary school, we pulled the cushions off the chairs and couch and did everything we could think of with them. We rode them down the stairs covered in wool, rose-colored carpet, built forts by turning them on their sides, and jumped on them from the arm of the couch.

Our best forts were the three-foot by three-foot by three-foot empty toilet paper boxes. Mother bought toilet paper a thousand rolls at a time from Dave Solomon. They came in a huge box and resided in the attic. If the box was nearly empty, we could put the remaining rolls on the floor of the attic and bring the box down to the living room. We usually cut windows in the box and draped blankets over it. We then crawled into the box and parted the blankets when we wanted to look out of a window.

The doorway between the living room and dining room had molding that you could grab with your fingertips and swing from like Tarzan and Jane. The object was to jump from the arm of the couch, catch the molding with your fingers, and land exactly in the middle of the cushions on the floor. We would get so hot, running and jumping, that we had to go outside to cool off.

Once on the porch, we would seize our bicycles and ride them around the porch for a few minutes and then ride them into the house because we were cold. The most common route was a simple circle around the maple dining room table with its six chairs. Sometimes one of us would get out our roller skates and skate around the table, chasing whomever was on a bicycle. The bicycles worked well on the wool carpet; the roller skates didn't work at all well. While the linoleum floors in the kitchen and laundry room were perfect for biking and skating, there simply wasn't enough space in these rooms for such activities.

If it happened to be a warm day (warm being a relative term, meaning that it was in the fifties), we would roller-skate or jump on our pogo stick from our house, past Ruth's, to Dick's. We always went in this direction because Ruth's sidewalk was macadam, whereas all the other sidewalks near us were made with large flagstones, separated by significant spaces.

One thing everyone knew was that we weren't allowed to throw a ball in the house. Mother treasured a milk-glass candy dish that was one of her wedding gifts. She frequently warned us that if we broke this, we would be in BIG trouble.

"I let you kids do almost anything you want in this house. But throwing a ball is one thing I will *not* tolerate. I really don't want any windows broken or the candy dish. Is that clear?" Mother said in her most serious tone of voice on many occasions.

The candy dish survived until Brian was sixteen. One day, he and his best friend Steve were home alone tossing a ball in the house. You know the rest—they broke the candy dish. Mother was very upset, to say the least. But she found someone to repair it and, much to Brian's and Steve's relief, the repair was almost impossible to see. This episode became a legend in our household. To this day, whenever any of us see Steve, the topic of the broken candy dish comes up. Several years later, Mother found and bought the exact same dish and gave it to Steve as a wedding gift.

April is also the month the *Titanic* sank. Grandma Cowan was fascinated by this event. Whenever the newspaper or *TIME* magazine had a story about it, she brought it to my attention.

"I remember one of our hired hands telling us what he had heard in town. He had gone to the store for some provisions in our horse and wagon. In the beginning, all we heard was that some big ship had gone down at sea and all of these very wealthy people were on it and they had all drowned. No one could believe it," Grandma said.

"Why didn't you listen to the radio?" I asked, knowing that television hadn't been invented yet.

"We didn't have a radio and no telephone, either," Grandma explained. "We just got a magazine or two and the local newspaper. I think the owner of the store heard about it from someone who delivered something to the store. The news was already four or five days old by the time we heard it up on the farm. We didn't go to town that often, you know."

I just couldn't believe what it must have been like to learn about newsworthy events many days later.

"Did you know that the ship was supposed to be unsinkable?" I said.

"We learned that after it went down. I think it was a good two or three weeks later that I finally believed all of those people had drowned. People in first class and people in steerage, just like we were when we came across the ocean," Grandma said.

"That's right. I forget that you came to America on a ship," I said.

"I could never get it out of my head that the band played 'Nearer, My God, to Thee' as the ship sank," Grandma said. "Those poor people."

I attribute my slightly more than casual interest in the *Titanic* to Grandma Cowan's vivid description of what it was like to learn about the April 10, 1912, sinking of the ship.

In retrospect, I should have asked her to come to school and tell my class about what it was like to learn of the sinking of the *Titanic.* I'm sure this never occurred to either my mother or me because Grandma Cowan was, to be blunt, just not very presentable and wouldn't have been very articulate before an audience, even a class of fourth graders.

While we never liked to admit it, we were always happy when school started again. These two-week April vacations were dumb, especially in a place like Fleischmanns that has so much more to do in winter when there is still snow on the ground.

Chapter 16

Relaxing Sundays

Brian and Dean skating on tennis courts with
Palace Hotel in background, 1965

During the school year, Sundays were nearly all
the same. We all got up, had breakfast, and we three
kids went to Sunday school. Fleischmanns had three
houses of worship: a synagogue, a Roman Catholic
Church, and a Methodist Church. We went to the
Methodist Church. We usually walked the half-mile or
so to church. Sunday school started at ten in the
morning and lasted until just before eleven, when
church started. For many years, Mother was a Sunday
school teacher. She felt she wasn't a good teacher. I
thought she was neither the best nor the worst.

I never really understood what we were taught in Sunday school. It was mostly too abstract for literal me. I'm a very concrete, show-me type of person. I suppose you would say that I am a born skeptic, and matters of faith escape my comprehension. I'm not against it; I just don't fully understand it. As my brother Brian says, "That's why they call it 'faith.'"

Mother, on the other hand, had a deep, abiding faith. When I was seven, I thought I'd have her faith by the time I was fifteen. When I was fifteen, I thought I'd have it by the time I finished college. When I finished college, I thought I'd have it when I was in my forties. Well, here I am in my sixties and still waiting. In the meantime, I have come to the conclusion that my assignment in life is to do unto others as I would have them do unto me.

Starting in seventh grade, I was the church organist. My predecessor had left for college to become a music teacher. I had taken piano lessons since first grade and was a slightly above-average pianist for our town. I also accompanied the junior high choir at school, so I was somewhat used to playing while others sang. Initially, my cousin Danny and I split organ-playing duty, but then he moved to Florida. This meant I had to go to Sunday school and church nearly every Sunday. I thought this would help me on my quest to "seeing the light." Besides, I got paid for being in church. Who else but the minister could say that?

The organ was on the altar and in full view of the congregation. So there was no hiding the fact that I was playing and all of those mistakes were mine. Quite an incentive to practice!

My mother signed me up for organ lessons from Mrs. Truran, the wife of the Methodist minister in Margaretville. Mrs. Truran was a wonderful teacher. I learned a lot from her. She selected great music for me to play as the prelude, the postlude, and while the collection was being taken. And then I had all those hymns to learn.

I usually walked to the church on Saturday afternoons to practice. Most of the time, practicing wasn't a problem. But in the dead of winter, it was quite a challenge. The sanctuary was probably all of fifty degrees, if that. Once there, I took off my big winter coat and mittens but left on my white wool hat. I played in old white sneakers because they slid over the pedals just right, and in the winter, I wore heavy, white athletic socks. I even wore the white socks during church because, even though the heat was on, the church didn't get very warm on the coldest of winter days. What a fashion statement I made in white sneakers, white wool socks, and pleated red-and-black-plaid skirt with its coordinating red sweater!

When I went to practice, I always dreaded taking off my toasty boots to put on my frozen sneakers. I had an electric heater that sat on the caned seat of a chair that was on my right side, as close to the organ as I could get it. I turned it up to high and held my sneakers in front of it for a little while to try to warm them up. It helped a small amount, but the cold of the soles always seeped up into my toes. I then adjusted the heater so the hot air blew on to the two rows of keys. I always tried to warm them up for a few minutes before starting to practice, but I never seemed to make much progress. The keys were cold and slippery. It was like hitting black and white ice cubes.

The bench was also cold, but somehow I could ignore that. Not surprisingly, my fingers got cold first. Initially I put them in front of the heater, but that never seemed to warm them as fast as tucking them in my armpits between my heavy, wool sweater and cotton turtleneck for several minutes. The first time or two of practicing in the cold, I put my fingers in my armpit next to my skin. What a shocking experience that was!

While warming my fingers, I would practice just the pedal parts of the music. This might seem practical, but it really was of limited use because I was slightly off balance. When the chill of the room started to creep through my sweater and my nose started to drip, I left and walked home. Often it was warmer outside than in the church. Needless to say, during the winter, I didn't learn much new music.

My main tendency was to play all of the hymns presto, that is, very fast. After church, Grandma Mayes and her friends would smile at me and say how nicely I had done. No complaints from that department. But on the way home, Mother frequently said, "Marilyn, we could hardly catch our breathe in 'Rock of Ages.' Can't you slow it down—just a little?"

"Oh Mother, you know I hate dirges."

Mother went to church nearly every Sunday and summarized the sermon for Dad over our Sunday dinner, which was usually between one and two in the afternoon. Usually Mother put pot roast or homemade corned beef on the stove or had chicken ready for the oven before leaving for church. Grandma Cowan would peel the potatoes while we were at church. Then Mother only had to cook a frozen vegetable, put the potatoes on to cook, and make the gravy when she got back from church.

If we had pot roast, I always ate it with Mother's homemade mustard pickles, which she kept in the coldest room of the cellar. We called the room the fruit cellar. The fruit cellar usually had Mother's homemade bread-and-butter pickles, home-canned tomatoes, homemade grape juice, and home-canned beef. In the late fall and winter, it also had two crocks of corned beef, made according to my father's Aunt Anna's recipe.

Mother made the corned beef in December, when she was sure the fruit cellar would stay cold. When she wanted to have corned beef for a meal, she usually assigned Brian the task of retrieving a chunk or two. By March, when Brian returned from the cellar with the corned beef, he announced, "Mom, do you know there is mold floating around in the corned beef?"

"Don't worry. It won't hurt you. I wash the meat well before cooking it," Mother always replied. Since Mother was a nurse, we seldom questioned her judgment on matters of health and, I must admit, we never got sick from eating the corned beef or anything else, no matter how much past its expiration date.

Mother also bought at least one fifty-pound bag of white potatoes every fall. The bag resided in the fruit cellar. Being of Scotch, English, Irish, and German descent, we had potatoes with every supper unless we had spaghetti with meat sauce, creamed dried beef on toast, chili with hard rolls or, on rare occasions, takeout Chinese brought home from Kingston.

Dad spent Sunday mornings at the mill going over the books and looking at the orders he had. He was the only person there, except for the man who tended the wood-fired boiler. Dad said he got a lot accomplished on Sunday mornings. But he promised Mother that if he ever got rid of the mill, he would join her in church.

After dinner, Mother and Dad would take a long nap and we kids would be left to our own devices. In the fall and spring, we rode our bikes, played baseball or football, or went roller-skating on the sidewalk wearing skates that had clips that fastened to our shoes when we turned a special key. In the winter, we went ice-skating, worked on individual projects, roller-skated around the dining room table a few times, or got into general mischief.

Brian was always taking something apart or building something. He made many model airplanes, built radios, and ordered rockets and rocket engines. We were fortunate to live across the street from the ballpark. It was the perfect place to set off the rockets. He read *Popular Mechanics, Popular Science,* and *Boys' Life* from cover to cover, often with a cat on his lap. He pored over catalogs. Then he would make his case for why he absolutely, positively needed a particular kit to build something.

I usually made fudge or popcorn balls according to Aunt Anna's recipe or sewed something. Not that I was a very good seamstress. My sewing efforts taught me some version of patience and humility; at least that's what Mother told me.

Dean could never sit still. In the fall and spring, he spent a lot of time pestering Brian. When he wasn't doing that, he was in the church basement with his very good friend Rick (one of our minister's sons) smoking, playing cards, and playing with a CB radio. In our house, Rick was known for saying to his mother one day when he was four or five years old, "All I hear about in this house is germs and God and I've never seen either one."

Sometimes Dean helped me in the kitchen. He stirred the fudge while I measured out the ingredients to make popcorn balls. One afternoon, we made taffy. We made two batches, peppermint and vanilla. I was pouring the second cooked batch onto waxed paper to cool and Dean was pulling some of the first batch. The phone rang and I answered it. Clearly Dean couldn't answer the phone since his hands were full of taffy. It was Rick. He asked if he could talk to Dean. When I relayed this question to Dean, he said, "Tell him I'm tied up at the moment and I'll have to call him back." Which is exactly what I did. This inside joke amused Dean and me for at least an hour.

In the winter, we spent a lot of time ice-skating on the rink that was right across from our house. While we sometimes went skating after school or even after dinner under the lights on weekdays, Sunday afternoons were our favorite times for skating.

The village of Fleischmanns made an ice-skating rink by flooding the two tennis courts at the ballpark. Charley Maxim and Harris were the two village employees who did all of the road and park maintenance for the village. One of their duties was placing sandbags around the edges of the tennis courts and, using fire hoses, flooding the courts to a depth of four or five inches. It would take a few days and several coats of water for the ice to completely cover the courts. The result, if done right, was a great skating rink. The water for flooding the tennis courts came from the village public water well that was located about twenty-five feet from the courts. The wellhead was located underground in an eight-foot by eight-foot by eight-foot cinderblock-lined tomb.

Dean loved to ice-skate. When he was quite young, he helped Charley and Harris with the rink. He learned how to turn on the well water and connect the hose, and perfected squirting the water on the courts so the ice would be as smooth as glass. Soon Charley and Harris would just set him up and leave to do other jobs. Around the age of fifteen, Dean got permission from our father, who was the village mayor, to go down into the well hole, connect the fire hose, and turn on the water all by himself. He spent hours at the ballpark getting the ice just right. The result was a wonderful skating rink.

Once the ice was thick enough to skate on, most of the kids in town showed up to skate. As Brian, Dean, and I grew, we needed new skates every year or so. After several years of skating and growing, we had assorted sizes of both hockey and figure skates. Mother, always aware that many other families weren't as fortunate as ours, kept our old skates so we could lend them to others. Our doorbell was always ringing with one kid or another asking, "Can I borrow the hockey skates I used last Sunday?" or "Do you still have the size four figure skates I used last year?"

Occasionally we went skating on a shallow pond at the mill. One day while skating there, my feet got very cold. They haven't been the same since. Mother was always buying me socks that she thought were especially warm, but they never made much difference. I even went through a phase where I put my sock-covered feet in plastic bags. I guess the theory was that some how the plastic would be a barrier to the cold air. It wasn't.

When the skating wasn't good or we were tired of it, we descended to the cellar to play with the model train that Brian and Dean had set up in the basement. It had an engine, a caboose, a cattle car, a flat car for things like logs, and one or two more cars. They had two sets of tracks with switches, so the train could take several routes. We all spent hours setting up the people, the railroad station, houses, trees, cows, sheep, and horses. Our favorite thing was to put a small white pill in the smoke stack of the engine and watch the smoke come out. I wonder how many seconds that acidic-smelling smoke took off of our lives? We then wondered if we too could make something that was chemically interesting.

So then we went to the laundry room, where we frequently mixed various household ingredients to make substances we were sure were poisonous. Adding almond-scented hand lotion, which smelled poisonous to us, would certainly make any mixture deadly. An optional ingredient was 20 Mule Team Borax, whose manufacturer sponsored the TV show *Death Valley Days*. Mother had both powdered and blocks of bluing. We usually used the powered, but sometimes we dunked the block in a measuring cup full of water if we thought our concoction would benefit by the addition of blue water. We frequently added Clorox and occasionally ammonia. In retrospect, we were lucky not to have died. No one told us about the dangers of mixing Clorox and ammonia. Good thing the laundry room was very large and somewhat drafty.

Sometimes we would simply sprinkle every substance we could find onto a sheet of paper, go out to the back porch, light a candle, and blow the substance across the flame. We tried sugar, baking soda, baking powder, laundry detergent, powdered bluing, salt, pepper, alum (which Mother used in making pickles), flour, baby powder, and everything else we could find.

We hit the jackpot when we gently blew flour across the flame of the candle. What a beautiful sight it made! The fine particles ignited with a whoosh and burned with every color of the rainbow. The lit particles spread out at least two feet beyond the paper. We had our own private fireworks display, right on our back porch. The show was best at night because it was very dark on the back porch. The colors were so bright.

While we kids were engaged in our chemistry experiments, Mother and Dad would be reading the paper and listening to their LP records of whole operas or Beethoven symphonies. LP records turned at the speed of thirty-three and one-third revolutions per minute and they had just been invented. My parents preferred them to their old seventy-eight records that turned at the speed of seventy-eight revolutions per minute.

Around six o'clock, we would all be hungry. We usually had tuna fish sandwiches, homemade bread-and-butter pickles, and hot chocolate, but sometimes we had Mother's home-canned beef. Mother did all of her canning using the hot-water-bath method, and I am still here to tell the tale. The canned beef tasted like pot roast with gravy, and I often had it over two slices of white bread.

When I asked Mother if it was safe to eat the canned beef, she replied, "Of course it's safe. How do you think we preserved beef when I was a child before much refrigeration and no freezers?

There was usually leftover dessert, but if we didn't have any dessert, we always had two five-gallon tubs of ice cream in the freezer. We always had chocolate. The other flavor was often whatever had been on sale: vanilla, strawberry, coffee, Neapolitan, butter pecan, or maple walnut. The chocolate went the fastest.

Around seven o'clock, we would get out the Bonanza Rummy game. All you need to play the game is a Bonanza Rummy board (or the list of the card combinations that are on the board), a deck of cards, and poker chips. Before each game, we carefully counted out the chips, making sure everyone started with the same number. After several rounds of play, someone would be out of chips and would have to borrow some from one or more other players. We always made a big deal of keeping track of who borrowed how many chips from whom. We sometimes discussed whether we would charge interest, but we almost never did.

One of the card combinations in the game is a hand of poker. Dad was a good card player and enjoyed Bonanza Rummy. He often got a sheepish grin on his face when one of us kids was betting all of our chips against him on the strength of our poker hand. He won the poker hand more often than I like to admit, and he always made us turn over whatever chips we had bet.

Often the game proceeded slowly because one or more players would be watching *Walt Disney's Wonderful World of Color* on TV. Around eight, out came the popcorn popper. We made real popcorn, the kind cooked in corn oil with real butter drizzled over it followed by good old-fashioned salt. Two or three times a year, Mother would send one of us to the fruit cellar for a jar of her homemade grape juice. She didn't make it every year, and all five of us would consume two quarts in an evening.

Grandma Cowan never participated in any of this activity. She was usually in bed by the time we started the popcorn maker and never liked playing games.

On Sundays, everyone but me went to bed by nine. I took my shower, put on my pajamas and robe, and came back downstairs to watch *Bonanza*. It was my favorite TV show and it was on from nine until ten. It was on the only channel we got, NBC, channel 6, out of Schenectady. I think we were lucky to get that station with the antenna that was on the roof of the house.

On Monday, Dad went to the mill, we kids went to school, and Mother did whatever stay-at-home mothers did in those years: cooked, cleaned, washed the clothes and hung them out on the line to dry, did the ironing, paid the bills, talked to her friends on the phone, took one grandmother or the other to the doctor, etc.

Chapter 17

School

Fleischmanns High School - elementary
classrooms in wooden part of building and high school
rooms in brick part, from 1966 yearbook

I liked school. I liked walking to school, except
when it was pouring or very cold, enjoyed being with
the same kids year in and year out, and liked walking
home. I liked nearly all of my teachers, and I think I
received a very good education even though there were
only sixteen of us in my class by senior year.

There were about 225 students in grades K–12.
My   father   and   his   sister   were   both   in   the

Fleischmanns High School class of 1938. Dad was in the same grade as his younger sister because he missed a year of school at age six.

Dad missed a year of school because the doctor said he had Saint Vitus Dance. (Saint Vitus Dance can occur after a certain type of strep infection and is characterized by involuntary and uncoordinated movements of a person's limbs and face.) The prescribed treatment was staying in bed for a year. The few times Dad spoke about this, he said he thought the doctor was wrong and being confined to bed was terrible. Whenever Grandma Mayes spoke about this she said, "Can you imagine? Who could keep a six-year-old in bed for a year?" As an active child, I agreed with them.

I was in the class of 1967. The class of 1968 was the last class to graduate from Fleischmanns High School. The next year, the school merged with Margaretville Central School. I have often told people that the school tried to operate after I left and, after just one year, discovered that it wasn't possible.

Kindergarten: Miss Estus

Kindergarten was a full-day affair. According to the yearbook, there were nineteen of us. The yearbook doesn't mention if anyone was absent the day the photo was taken. I certainly don't remember.

Since I had had polio the summer before I went to kindergarten (the vaccine wasn't yet in use), I went for only half a day for a month or two. I am very fortunate to have no paralysis.

We started every morning with the principal of the whole school making announcements over the loudspeaker. When the announcements were over, we all stood up and put our right hand over the left side of our chest as he (yes, the principals were always men) led the whole school in the Pledge of Allegiance.

One of my first acts was biting my friend Cathy on the arm the first day of school. We were lining up to go outside for recess and I wanted to be first in line. Guess sharing wasn't yet in my repertoire. I think this was my last act of physical aggression, except for pounding on my brothers when we fought.

We learned the names of the colors. Miss Estus made large rectangles of each primary color on the blackboard using colored chalk. When she was helping one kid, another went to the blackboard and erased the green rectangle. Being ever helpful, I went up to the blackboard and made a new green rectangle—using my green crayon. Miss Estus yelled at me. She thought I did the whole thing.

I tried to explain I was trying to repair the damage someone else had done. This was the first time someone unjustifiably questioned my veracity. It was a shocking experience.

Then there was naptime. I didn't need a nap but I loved pulling out the navy-blue cots and covering up in my mostly red and green, cotton-flannel blanket. The most fun came when naptime was over. Everyone found a partner and each person took two corners of a blanket. Then, to fold it in half, each person ran into his or her partner, bumping chests. The whole thing was repeated until the blanket was the right size to put away. To this day, my husband and I fold sheets and blankets using this method, although usually without the bumping part.

First Grade: Mrs. Thompson

Mrs. Thompson was old, very old, and thin. At least that is how she seemed to me. She was very strict, but I didn't fear her. If a kid misbehaved, her favorite disciplinary tactic was to grab the kid on the arm between the elbow and the armpit. She squeezed the arm with her bony thumb on one side and fingers on the other until the muscles were pressed against the bone. It hurt! I didn't have this done to me more than once or twice. I think some kids did.

We still took naps in first grade. We frequently ate small pieces of the white paper that had wrapped the straws we used to drink our milk at lunch. The paper was on the floor, and since we were so close to the floor when we were on the cots, one or another of the boys in class would dare us to eat some. It took forever to get it moist enough to swallow. The largest number of pieces I ever ate at one naptime was four.

We learned to read from those famous books about Dick and Jane and their dog Spot. Even in the first grade, "See Jane run. Look. Look at Jane run" was boring.

The plots to the stories were thin, to say the least. I remember counting the number of letters in the words I had learned, and remember when the longest word I knew was "sometimes."

When it was time to learn to read, Mrs. Thompson had us sit in a circle and take turns reading out loud. The children who had trouble with reading on a particular day went to remedial reading taught by Mrs. Reynolds. Everyone in school loved Mrs. Reynolds. Not only did she teach remedial reading, she also was an assistant cook in the cafeteria.

One day, one of my friends said, "Let's read really bad today so we can go to remedial reading. Those kids seem to have a lot of fun."

"Okay," I said.

Well, my friend read first and did very poorly. I hate to admit it, but by the time my turn came, I chickened out. When my friend was told she had to go to remedial reading, she cried. She tried to explain that she had read poorly on purpose.

When she got back from remedial reading, she said it was a lot of fun and she wanted to go again. So the next day, she read poorly again. But Mrs. Thompson didn't send her. Then my friend cried because she couldn't go to remedial reading. Such were the traumas of first grade.

The summer before first grade, Grandma Mayes bought my cousin Danny and me each a piano. So after school started, I started piano lessons. I took them for years from Mrs. Place, who lived in Margaretville. For the most part, I loved playing the piano.

That spring, Dean was born.

Second Grade: Mrs. Birdsall

I absolutely loved Mrs. Birdsall. She really understood children. We learned how to add and subtract two-digit numbers. When we arrived in the morning, the day's math problems were already on the blackboard. For most of second grade, I wondered how they got there.

It wasn't until spring that I discovered how the problems got on to the blackboard. One day, I had just started my walk home when I realized I had left my sweater at my desk. I went back to get it and there was Mrs. Birdsall putting the next day's math problems on the blackboard. How clever. *So she doesn't come in extra early to do that,* I thought.

During the winter of second grade, my father was close to having a nervous breakdown, or at least that is what Mother explained to me years later. The doctor recommended that he take a long vacation from the business; so my parents, Brian, and I went to Florida for about six weeks. Dean stayed with Aunt Gerry, Uncle Jim, and Danny.

I had wanted to see Dean learn to walk, but he learned while we were in Florida. I have always regretted this.

We rented an apartment and went to the ocean nearly every day. While I thought the water was warm, our neighbor, who was a full-time resident of Florida, told me that only northerners went swimming in the winter.

This same neighbor was retired and he spent a large portion of his day sitting on his porch steps keeping track of the make and year of each car that went by. He had daily totals for each car model. One day, he said to me, "Does your dad count cars?"

"No," I said, thinking, *Little does he know that my dad doesn't even know one kind of car from another, except for the color.*

Early grade school was the era of air-raid drills and bomb shelters. Our family didn't have a bomb shelter. In fact, I don't think anyone in Fleischmanns did. But they certainly were a big topic in the news, which we were forced to listen to every weekday at dinner.

Sometimes during an air-raid drill at school, we had to go into the hall, stand with our foreheads touching the wall and our hands lapped one over the other above our heads. The idea was that our hands would keep the falling debris out of our faces. We stood there for what seemed like an hour, though I now assume it was more like ten to fifteen minutes. Other times, we were told to go under our desks for protection.

I never understood why the rules changed or how we kids were supposed to know what to do, especially if a bomb really did hit near Fleischmanns. I always figured that the Russians wouldn't really aim for Fleischmanns. The most likely scenario would be that Fleischmanns would be hit because the Russians were aiming for New York City and missed—by a very long shot.

After telling my parents one evening at dinner about that day's air-raid drill, Mother said, "Well, if they drop an atom bomb, I sure hope my family and I go in the first attack."

I remember thinking, *It is okay for you to wish that for yourself, but you can leave me out of that wish.*

Third Grade: Mrs. Morse

Mrs. Morse was a very good teacher.

As startling as it seems now, Mrs. Morse started every morning with the whole class saying the Lord's Prayer, the Protestant version. As far as I know, no one ever complained, even though I had both Jewish and Roman Catholic classmates.

In third grade, as in all the other grades, we loved receiving mimeographed handouts. The odor from the paper was one of our favorite smells. Every time we received a handout, we all immediately put the paper as close to our nose as possible and inhaled deeply, several times. I wonder if mimeographed paper would be banned as dangerous to our health today.

During grade school, recess was outside unless it was raining. Then it was in the gym, where we played dodgeball—a great game that honed both our ability to throw accurately and move out of the way quickly.

In third grade, when we came in from recess, Mrs. Morse read to us. Our favorite book was Laura Ingalls Wilder's *Little House on the Prairie*. In fact, everyone enjoyed the story so much she read at least one of Laura Ingalls Wilder's other books to us.

Fourth Grade: Mrs. Craft

My biggest memory of fourth grade is of our teacher, Mrs. Craft, saying, "I hear noise" as I was trying to concentrate while taking a test, any and every old test. The whole room could be as quiet as a tomb and Mrs. Craft would announce in a rather loud voice, "I hear noooooiiiise."

I would think, *If you would be quiet, there wouldn't be any noise.*

She sent kids who misbehaved to the cloakroom. The classroom had an old-fashioned cloakroom where you hung up your coat and left your boots. I don't remember ever being sent there.

Fourth grade was the grade our school allowed children to be dismissed early one afternoon a week during the winter so they could take ski lessons at Belleayre Ski Center. The ski center offered lessons and rented the equipment at reduced rates. While a few of my classmates signed up for these lessons in fourth grade, I didn't sign up until seventh grade. I always regretted waiting until seventh grade.

Fourth grade was the year the Roman Catholic kids were excused early one afternoon a week to go to the Roman Catholic Church in Margaretville to learn their catechism, whatever that was. I never knew what they learned; they never wanted to talk about it.

This was the grade when you could sign up to learn an instrument in school. I, or more accurately Mother, picked the flute because we already had one. Mother had played the flute in high school. She couldn't play it very well, but it was something that we had in the attic.

Miss Boyden was the music teacher for the whole school: all bands, all choirs, all music classes, and all instrument lessons. In this regard, the music teacher was just like the coach who was responsible for gym for grades K–12; junior varsity basketball, varsity basketball, and baseball, if the school had a team that year.

The flute was the instrument Miss Boyden played, and she was a very good teacher. At the time, the village hired the school music teacher for the summer so the village could have summer band concerts on the porch of the library. In the summer, I went to the school once a week for flute lessons and once or twice a week for elementary school band practice.

At my flute lessons, Miss Boyden taught me the very basics of how to conduct in 4/4 time and in 3/4 time. She told me to practice this at home, which I did. Then, at one of the concerts at the library, she asked me to conduct the next piece.

Boy, was I surprised! I never guessed that this was why she was teaching me the basics of conducting. I protested that I didn't think I knew enough to conduct a whole piece and said, "Who is going to play my part? I'm first chair flute and there is a solo in this piece."

Miss Boyden said, "I'll play your part." And, knowing she would do a very good job, I was stuck trying to figure out some other objection.

While I was thinking the situation over, she asked the other members of the band if they wanted me to conduct. They said, "Yes."

That chorus of yeses from the other members of the band shocked me. *Don't they know any better?* Now I knew I was stuck. There was no way out.

So the next thing I knew, I was in front of the whole band waving my arms. Miss Boyden hadn't told my parents this might happen. So they too were taken aback when they saw me up there conducting.

After the concert, I met my parents on the sidewalk across the street from the library.

"Marilyn, we nearly missed seeing you conduct. We were so busy visiting with Ann and Bill. It's a good thing you wore your blue fish dress," Mother said.

"You did very well," Dad said with a big smile on his face.

My blue fish dress figured prominently in another big event in my life: my first date with my best friend Dick, who, as you'll remember, is three years older than I.

One morning that same summer, Dick rang our doorbell. "Mare, want to go on a date? Let's go to the movies this afternoon."

"No, I'd rather play baseball. What's playing, anyway?"

"*The King and I*. It's really good. Let's go. I'll pay and everything."

"Well, okay."

"Be sure to wear that blue dress of yours with the fish on it. I really like that dress. I'll be here to pick you up at one thirty. Remember, I'll pay for everything."

Dick was right. *The King and I* was a wonderful movie. But I really wasn't interested in this dating stuff. I'd rather play baseball.

Fifth Grade: Mrs. Kittle

Mrs. Kittle had taught fifth grade forever. Boy, did she know her stuff. She was very firm, but very fair. She thought every child could learn what she was teaching, if they only worked a little bit. She was more than willing to give them whatever assistance they needed.

The most shocking thing that happened in fifth grade was that the boys would occasionally capture flies and take their wings off before killing them. Horrid, I know.

It was around fifth grade that I became aware of just how poor some families in the area were. I remember going to visit Grandma Mayes's sister Anna and her husband Charles Morse in Halcott[2] one winter day to go sledding. Uncle Charles and Aunt Anna were retired dairy farmers. They still lived on the farm and rented their hayfields to other farmers. One field was across the road from their house. It had a long, steep hill and, after a snowstorm, was a perfect place for using the large, aluminum, shallow bowl-shaped disks we called "flying saucers." Once or twice a winter, after Sunday dinner, our parents drove the twenty minutes it took to get to Aunt Anna's.

---

[2] Pronounced haw-kit, with the emphasis on "haw." It's a dead giveaway that a person isn't from the area if he or she asks how to get to "hall-cot."

Mother would call Aunt Anna before going to church to ask if it was okay for us to come up that afternoon. Aunt Anna nearly always said yes.

Before getting in the car to go there, Dad went to the attic to get a bottle of Canadian Club whiskey. As we got in the car he said to Mother, "I have a bottle of Canadian Club for Uncle Charles, I'm sure he can't afford to buy it and he always seems to enjoy having a drink with me when we get there."

Once at Aunt Anna's, we immediately piled out of the car, retrieved our equipment from the trunk, and we kids ran across the road to go sledding while our parents went into the house. After about an hour, we would be cold and wet, so we went into the house. We always entered through the kitchen, took off our boots and snowsuits, and made ourselves at home in the living room, which was always way too hot; it must have been eighty-eight degrees in there. Beads of sweat would form all over my body, followed by a chill.

Aunt Anna nearly always served us her famous popcorn balls, made with molasses, butter, and a little vinegar. Mmmm.

On our way to and from Aunt Anna's, we always went past two old buses where two families lived. The families had children who were only a little older than I. I couldn't imagine how cold it must be in a bus, especially at night, even if they did have some type of wood-burning stove. Mother said she thought they got their water from a nearby stream. *No wonder their clothes aren't as clean as mine*, I thought.

I remember seeing these children in school the next day and wondering exactly what their life was like at home. I felt sorry for them. I knew their life was very different from mine.

Sixth Grade: Mrs. Zusselman

Mrs. Zusselman and her husband had recently moved to Fleischmanns, so all of us were new to her. When she took attendance on the first day of class, she came across the name of one of our classmates who was absent: Dennis. As soon as she called his name several of us shouted, "He won't be here until the end of September. He's still with the carnival."

"He's where?" Mrs. Zusselman said.

"On the road with the carnival. We can't wait for him to get back. Class is so much more exciting when he is here," one of the boys shouted from the back of the room.

Every Monday for the first few weeks, Mrs. Zusselman would look around to see if anyone new was in class and then inquire when Dennis would be back. One day she told us that she had gone to the office to make sure we had been telling the truth. She said she had begun to doubt us.

Dennis finally showed up and, true to his reputation, kept the class entertained with stories of his adventures of being on the road. He had experienced things most of us knew about only from reading books.

Sixth grade is when I learned something about speaking up for myself. When the sixth grade went to gym class, the classroom was used as a study hall for some of the high school kids. That year, I switched over to using mechanical pencils instead of regular wooden pencils. Dad always used a mechanical pencil and I thought I'd give it a try. I liked my pencil because I never had to sharpen it, it was round so there were no edges to make dents in my finger, and I only had to keep it filled with extra lead and keep an extra eraser on hand.

One day, when I returned from gym, I looked in my desk for my black mechanical pencil. It was gone. I raised my hand immediately and told Mrs. Zusselman that it was missing. She told me the name of the senior boy who had sat at my desk and suggested I go to the office to find out what classroom he was in, then go to that classroom and ask to see him to see if he had my pencil.

Oh no, I thought. *She expects me to confront this senior who's the largest teenager in the school.* I was tall for my age, but he was a lot taller, probably at least six feet tall, and he was big and strong.

I was in a pickle. I really wanted my pencil back, and now everyone knew what I had been instructed to do about it.

So off I went down the steps to the office. It was a very short walk. *Maybe June, the secretary, will offer to go with me and, more important, talk to the boy, once I explain my situation.* After explaining the situation to June, she looked in a book and told me the boy was in English class.

What, no offer of help? Well, the phone was ringing and I did realize that she was too busy to go, even if it had occurred to her. So off I went to the room where all of the English classes were held.

I knocked on the door and the English teacher answered it. I asked for the boy and the English teacher summoned him. The boy stood in the doorway while I stood in the hall. He towered over me.

"Do you have my black mechanical pencil?" I said.

"No," he said.

"Well, what's that behind your ear?" I said pointing to his left ear and trembling inside.

"Oh, I forgot I had that," he said as he removed it and handed it to me.

"Thanks," I said, feeling a great sense of relief.

When I entered my classroom, I smiled and held up my hand with my pencil in it.

Seventh and Eighth Grades (Junior High):

In seventh grade, there were nineteen of us, fourteen of whom had been with me since kindergarten. So when I say I knew, as in really truly knew, my classmates, it is true.

One of the privileges that started in seventh grade was, if you got a note from home, you could leave the school grounds and go to Main Street, a.k.a. over-street, at lunchtime. My friends and I walked through the school playground, across a footbridge, and down a short alley to Main Street nearly every day after lunch. We usually went to Muller's store and bought licorice, fireballs, bubble gum, or button-sized sugar dots that came in several colors and were stuck to white paper the size of cash register tape. The total cost of our purchases was usually five cents. Sometimes I splurged and bought seven or eight cents' worth of candy.

We each had a locker in the hall and changed both classrooms and teachers for each course. New York State required girls to take Home Economics and boys to take Shop. The boys went to Margaretville Central School on the bus for Shop.

The most memorable thing about Home Ec was the day one of my classmates used the sewing machine for the first time. She didn't know enough to take her foot off the pedal to stop the machine. She just threw up her hands and screamed, "Make it stop! Make it stop!" Eventually, between the kids and the teacher yelling at her to take her foot off the pedal, she did get the machine to stop.

Needless to say, a few years later when it came time to drive the car as part of our driver's education class, this episode was mentioned nearly every time the girl got behind the wheel. Some things are hard to live down.

I was still taking piano lessons from Mrs. Place in Margaretville. Brian and Dean took lessons from her, as well. The drill was: Mother picked us up on Fridays at the school and we made a beeline, as she called it, to Margaretville. She dropped the three of us off at Mrs. Place's while she went to Bussy's to do the weekly grocery shopping and to the Margaretville Bakery for jelly-filled donuts covered with confectioners' sugar, hard rolls, éclairs, and cookies.

We were done with our lessons at just about the same time Mother was done with the shopping. She would be starved on the way home and eat a jelly-filled donut while driving. She nearly always dropped some jelly on her coat or dress, saying, "I wish I didn't like these so much. They are so messy to eat in the car."

When we got home, we all toted the groceries into the house. Mother started dinner and we kids were assigned the task of putting away the groceries. We usually had pancakes and sausage, bacon and eggs, or homemade chili that Mother had defrosted earlier in the day with fresh hard rolls.

While Dean and I were busy putting away the groceries, Brian *always* had to go to the bathroom. He *always* stayed in the bathroom until Dean and I were done putting away the groceries. It took Dean and me more years than I like to admit to catch on to what was happening. Eventually, we just left a few boxes of groceries for him to put away.

High School

Of all of the classes I have taken in my life, the best one so far is Earth Science. I use my Earth Science knowledge nearly every day. Earth Science is where I learned that if a low-pressure front is approaching, there is a good chance of rain or snow and if a high-pressure front is stuck over me, it is likely to be nice for a while. Learning a little geology and about the solar system was also very interesting. Pluto was still one of the planets in the solar system back then.

On Friday, November 22, 1963, I was in ninth grade and looking forward to going home for the weekend in an hour or two. I had just gotten the books for my next class out of my locker and was in the green-tiled hall going to my next class when I heard someone say, "The President has been shot!"

I went to my next class and everyone was talking. Soon the principal made an announcement over the loudspeaker. He told us there were news reports that President Kennedy had been shot and that school was ending for the day. Needless to say, I watched TV the rest of that day and for the next three days.

I remember turning on the TV early the following Sunday afternoon and seeing Lee Harvey Oswald, President Kennedy's assassin, being shot by Jack Ruby as Oswald was being escorted by the police to go to another facility. I have never understood how the police let that happen.

We didn't have school the following Monday, the day of President Kennedy's funeral. The two things that I saw that day that caught my attention the most were the horse with no rider but with boots in the stirrups that faced backward and the eternal flame at Kennedy's gravesite.

Then there were the race riots. I remember seeing pictures of large portions of cities, usually the poorer sections, going up in flames. The riots went on day after day around the country. Since I lived in an all-white small village in the north, I had no real idea what the problems were that led to the riots. It seemed crazy to me that some places had rules about where people could sit on a bus or who could sit at a lunch counter. The fact there were such rules was all news to me.

In ninth grade, I became addicted to *The New York Times*. Throughout high school, I bought the paper for five cents a day. Every Monday, I gave the boy who sold the paper a quarter. My friends Ronnie and Steve (the same Steve I went skiing with) also bought the paper, and we spent hours reading and discussing what we had read. It was during one of these discussions that Ronnie announced his theory of how to know whether the stock market would go up or down. The market followed the price of bacon. Yes, that is what this Jewish boy, whose home I'm sure didn't have a slice of bacon in it, announced. Steve and I just laughed.

While we were in homeroom and before discussing that day's *Times*, Ronnie reenacted Johnny Carson's monologue from the prior evening's *Tonight Show*. Nearly the whole class listened. He did a wonderful job entertaining us every morning. And reading the *Times* helped immensely in understanding Carson's monologue. No wonder I loved going to school.

Mr. Rubin, our English teacher, sometimes read stories to us from *The New York Times* as part of our class. During the spring of 1964, the class followed the story of the murder of Kitty Genovese, an event that vividly comes to my mind even today. Kitty was a twenty-eight-year-old woman who was murdered in a quiet neighborhood in Queens while about thirty-eight people watched and did nothing. They didn't even call the police even though Kitty cried out for help.

My math teacher for grades seven through eleven was Mrs. Taber. She was a wonderful teacher. We had homework problems nearly every day and graded our own papers the next day. One day, Mrs. Taber told us that a parent complained to her that some students cheated when they graded their own papers. The parent wanted her to have students exchange papers. Mrs. Taber told us she replied, "What difference does it make if math is the only class a person passes?" So we continued to grade our own papers and I continued to think she was a wonderful teacher. In eleventh grade, I took trigonometry and scored one hundred on the New York State Regents Exam. I was so happy. The day I found out, I told Dad my accomplishment at dinner.

He smiled and replied with what he nearly always said whenever someone bragged about themselves, "My, how we apples do swim." By then he didn't have to explain his Grandmother Maggie Mayes's saying to me.

The story behind the saying is that there are several apples and one pile of horse manure swimming in a puddle after a rainstorm. The pile of manure looks around and says to the apples, "My, how we apples do swim."

I wasn't a cheerleader and there were no sports for girls. So, my main extra-circular activities revolved around music. I was the piano accompanist for the junior high and high school choirs and played the flute in the band. I had a love–hate relationship with the flute. I liked being in the high school band. We sounded so much better than the elementary school band. I totally loved playing in our Christmas and spring concerts and enjoyed the marching part of being in parades. But since I couldn't memorize music (or anything else), playing the flute and trying to read music while marching was extremely frustrating. There were two types of contraptions I could use to hold the music while marching. One went around my neck and the other went under my left arm. First I would try one and then switch to the other. Neither was satisfactory. They both bounced horridly when I marched, making it impossible to read the music. After a week of total frustration I often announced to Mother that I was ready to give up the flute. She always told me to wait a few weeks. Of course, by then, the parade was over and the band was practicing for a concert, something I liked.

The main parade we played in was the annual Memorial Day parade. It started at the school and ended in front of the library. There were a few speeches, a prayer, and the playing of "Taps" by one of the band's trumpet players. He played it from the hill behind the library. This part was always haunting and powerful.

The worst part of the Memorial Day parade was how hot we sometimes got. The school bought heavy, wool uniforms and, surprisingly, sometimes it was actually quite warm in Fleischmanns on Memorial Day. In fact, one year, one of the very thin girls in band fainted dead away because she was got overheated. Of course, other years there was frost in our yard when we got up on Memorial Day.

Some of my classes during senior year were minuscule. I was essentially going to an elite public school. I just didn't realize it. Only three of us took French four, physics and math four.

During spring break our senior year, we took a class trip to Washington, D.C. The class had had fund-raising events throughout high school so we would have enough money to pay for a large portion of the trip. Nearly the whole class went. We went by bus, stayed in a hotel, and saw the sights. It was a wonderful trip.

I loved Moving-Up Day. It was held near the end of the school year. We played various sports in the morning and went to an assembly in the afternoon where the principal handed out various awards.

Each year, my father's company gave the student who achieved the highest score on any math Regents a monetary prize. I know I won the prize in eleventh grade and at least one other time, maybe two. It was a little embarrassing to claim the prize and sometimes kids teased me that the "fix was in," but I knew I had earned the prize honestly.

The first year I was in college, Brian won the prize. When his name was called, the principal said, "So, I see we are keeping with the Mayes tradition of keeping the math prize in the family."

Aside from the monetary prizes, the best part of Moving-Up Day was the end. The high school kids sat in chairs, by grade, on the floor of the auditorium. The seniors sat in the front row of chairs. We all sang

"Where, Oh Where," the Moving-Up Day song, the first stanza of which is

> Where, oh where, are the grand old Seniors?
> Where, oh where, are the grand old Seniors?
> Where, oh where, are the grand old Seniors?
> Safe   now   in   the   wide,   wide   world.
>
> They've   gone   out   from   their   Alma   Mater,
> They've   gone   out   from   their   Alma   Mater,
> They've   gone   out   from   their   Alma   Mater,
> Safe now in the wide, wide world.

When we sang this stanza, the senior class walked up to the seats on the stage. This is where they would all be on graduation day.

After this, Moving-Up Day activities came to an end and I just walked home with a friend or two discussing the day's activities.

Albert Koutz, 1935. Grandma Cowan's father
who emigrated to U.S. with his family in 1890.

Andrew and Grandma (Anna) Cowan wedding
photo, 1909

Koutz siblings: Julius Koutz
Emma Southard, Bertha Koutz, and Grandma
(Anna) Cowan, 1964
Their mother's family had reunions.

Grandma (Nellie) Mayes and her sisters Anna
Morse, Gladys O'Brien, and Inez Jenkins, 1967

My mother, Bertha Cowan Mayes, on Cowan
family farm, 1925

Four generations of Mayeses: Harrison (Hat),
Howard, Victor, and Murray, 1928

My parents, Bertha and Murray Mayes, on
their wedding day, June 12, 1948

Me, 1950

Brian, **1953**

Dean, 1957

Brian and Grandma Cowan in our backyard,
1952

Me and my best friend Dick in my backyard,
1953

My cousin Danny and me, 1953

My cousin Danny and me at Halloween in my
living room, 1954

Me, 1956. You can see Ruth Carey's porch, then
Dick's house with Park Terrace Hotel across from
Dick's.

Me and Brian making a snow cave, 1958

Brian about to enter backyard pool, 1958

My cousin Janet on her family farm in Ohio,
1959. She and her parents visited us every summer.

Dean in backyard, 1962. He always "accidently"
squirted the clothes Mother hung out to dry.

My cousin Danny, 1964

Our yellow cat, 1965. One of my favorite cats.

Brian reading on front porch with feet on
Cowan cobbler's bench, 1966

My parents, 1966

Standing: Dean, Me, and Brian
Seated: My parents, 1966. At Grandma Cowan's
house in New Kingston, NY.

Fleischmanns Methodist Church bazaar in
early 1970s. Sue Barrett in center in hat. "Go
fish" no longer conducted.

Grandma Mayes's casket in our dining room,
1974

Family reunion, 1976

Aunt Elsa Sanford with her children, 1982.
Back row: Doug, Dennis, and Lindie. Front row: Ruth,
Elsa and Elaine. Taken when Elsa was inducted into
Quilter's Hall of Fame.

Family reunion in our backyard, 1983

Croquet in our backyard at family reunion,
1983. Note the icehouse.

My parents on our back porch at the family
reunion, 1983. They frequently held hands.

Dry Brook stream where we nearly drown

Fleischmanns Methodist Church, 2013

Halcott Methodist Church, 2013

Ruth Carey's house and our "pine" tree, 2013

Me with my six-shooter and favorite outfit, 1954

Brian by quince bush, 1956

Brian dressed as a girl, 1956

Brian's birthday with Mother, Brian, Dean
(peering over a boy) and cousin Danny (standing), 1958

Me in my favorite blue, fish dress with
Grandma Mayes, 1959. I still have the dress!

Our backyard showing the roses. The bare spot
in foreground is second base, 1959

Dean, 1966 school photo. Just as I remember
him!

Brian, Grandma Cowan, Me, and Dean, 1967

Brian's jeep with Dean driving, 1970

My wedding, 1971

Bonanza Rummy board, Dad's Monopoly game,
Flinch, photo 2013

Mother's great-uncle's Carrom board.
photo 2013

Grandma Cowan's mother's spinning wheel
with mittens knit by Grandma Cowan, photo 2013

Cowan family cherry table made in early 1800s,
photo 2013

Chapter 18

Shopping in Oneonta

Map of New York drawn by me, 2013

Once or twice a year, Mother would say to Dad at dinner, "I think it's time we all go clothes shopping. The kids need a few things, I could use a new dress to wear to church, and I notice that you could use a new pair of dress pants and a new sport coat. We don't have anything going on this Saturday. Do you want to go to Kingston or Oneonta?"

"Let's go to Oneonta," Dad usually replied.

By the time I was twelve, as soon as these discussions began, memories of car sickness invaded my brain. I felt nauseous just thinking about being in the car for the trip to Oneonta. It was at the very limit of my tolerance for morning car trips over winding roads. And all roads out of Fleischmanns in those days followed one winding stream or another.

I usually made it to Oneonta without asking Mother or Dad to stop to let me vomit, but that was never guaranteed. Since Kingston was closer, I usually hoped that his choice would be Kingston. Unless, of course, it was summer. In that case, I hoped for Oneonta because it was cooler than hot old Kingston. If we went to Kingston and we knew it was going to be hot, we sometimes put a plastic container filled with ice cubes in a cooler, so we could eat the ice cubes in the car. At the time, most cars, including ours, didn't have air conditioning. On hot days, I was always glad when we gained altitude on our way home from Kingston and the air coming in through the car windows was cool at last.

Since Dad had gone to college in Oneonta, he liked that city. Also, Bresee's Department Store had a nice selection of classical music records, which he liked. In many ways, Dad was just like a teenager driven to buy and listen to the music he liked best.

If it was winter and some snow had just fallen or we had had a small ice storm, the conversation invariably turned to which route to take. We could go through Stamford, which was flatter and would take a little longer, or we could go through Delhi and over Franklin Mountain. Franklin Mountain was noted for its steepness and poor road conditions.

I always hoped for Franklin Mountain, the shorter and more scenic route. Sometimes we went one way and returned the other.

Kingston was the least challenging of all (except for the trip over Pine Hill), since it was south of us and the mountains were more rolling. But Mother and Dad seldom changed our destination because of weather.

Dad always drove and Mother sat in the front passenger's seat. She chatted the whole way there and the whole way home. Occasionally one or the other of us spoke up, but it wasn't at all necessary. Mother always brought along miniature candy bars for us to munch on and usually some fruit. If apples were in season, she brought them, along with a paring knife and some paper towels. She always quartered, cored, and peeled the apples for Dad and handed them to him as he drove. Dad didn't like the skin of any fruit. He even spit out grape skins.

"Bertha, can you unwrap a Baby Ruth for me?" Dad asked as he drove, even though it was only eight thirty in the morning.

Mother unwrapped the candy bar and extended her hand toward Dad. He would have to take his eyes off the road to find it. Mother, on the other hand, had her eyes glued to the road.

"Watch out, Murray, there's a car coming," Mother would say as her hand went up to control the steering wheel.

"Just put the candy bar in my hand. That way I can watch the road."

"I can't. I have to keep my eyes on the road," Mother would illogically reply.

"But I'm the driver," Dad would logically point out.

Eventually we arrived in Oneonta. We always parked right behind Bresee's Department Store. As we piled out of the car, Mother and Dad discussed what time we would meet for lunch. We usually had lunch at Bresee's lunch counter, but sometimes we went to another restaurant within walking distance of the store.

As soon as we arrived, Dad made a beeline to the record department. He was in heaven. They allowed customers to play the records on record players that were located in soundproof booths.

Dad spent the rest of the morning there. Sometimes we had to go get him because he didn't show up at the appointed hour for lunch.

In the meantime, Mother and the three of us kids went shopping for whatever it was she said we needed. We got most of our clothes and shoes in Oneonta or Kingston. Occasionally we ordered clothing from the Montgomery Ward catalog, but my experience was that I had to return most of the clothing because it wasn't made to fit my very long arms and legs. Dresses never fit no matter where I tried to buy them, because the waist was at least three inches above mine. If we went to Oneonta or Kingston, after much searching, I was usually able to find something that fit. These experiences made clothes shopping so traumatic that to this day I avoid it.

Bresee's lunch counter had the best club sandwiches ever served. When Brian and Dean were teenagers, they always ordered two turkey club sandwiches on white toast for lunch. On more than one occasion, the waitress brought only one club sandwich. But that mistake didn't take long to correct. The waitresses always explained that almost no one ordered two club sandwiches. The waitresses were always shocked when my brothers cleaned their plates. Not even a potato chip remained.

For dessert, Brian always had apple pie with a side of chocolate ice cream. Invariably, the pie came with vanilla ice cream, even though he emphasized chocolate when he placed the order.

After lunch, Mother would remind Dad that he too needed to get some new clothes. Once he got in either the men's section of Bresee's or went to a store that sold only men's clothing, he actively participated in choosing and trying on clothes. Dad liked to look nice and he always did.

We often had an early dinner in Oneonta before driving home.

I always enjoyed these family outings, even though Mother tried to drive the whole time, but never from behind the wheel.

Chapter 19

Looking Out for One Another

Fleischmanns library and Memorial Day
parade, 1962

AT THE POST OFFICE

One of Mother's good friends was Eva. She was
the wife of Jim, the postmaster. One winter day at
dinner, Mother laughed and said, "You can't believe
what Eva told me today. They all were eating dinner
last night and the phone rang. It was Peggy. She
walked by the post office while going to her apartment
and saw a ten- or eleven-year-old boy locked up in
there, banging on the window.

"Jimmy went right down and unlocked the post office to let Sammy out. Apparently, he had been curled up under the table in the lobby right by the radiator, reading his book. He was so engrossed in his book that he didn't realize Jimmy was locking up the post office. And Jimmy never thought to look under the table."

"I can believe it," Brian, who was in fifth grade, said. "He really doesn't know what is going on around him if he is reading. And he's always reading."

WATCHING OUT FOR OUR MORALS

Rose Green was a middle-aged lady who was the librarian and village clerk for years. She was also the self-appointed censor. She didn't allow adolescents to take out library books she thought were inappropriate. Even if the child had a note from his or her mother, Rose didn't always bend. She took her job very seriously.

In tenth grade, my friend Ronnie showed several of us a note allegedly from his mother saying he could take a certain book out of the library. He had written the note and forged his mother's signature. He said the book had some great sex in it and that Rose hadn't let him take it out the day before. After school, he was stopping at the library with his note.

He knew about the book from talking to guests at his parents' hotel. In fact, he had read several books like this one because guests had left them lying around. His parents didn't care what he read. They were just pleased he was reading.

The next day, we asked him if he was able to take the book out.

"Yeah. But, Rose detected the forgery and called my mother." He then said that his mother told Rose to go ahead and let him take out the book. She didn't care what her son read. She was just grateful he was going to the library at all.

We all thought his mother was one of the neatest ladies around.

Chapter 20

Youth Employment

Dad's office building attached to longer building where we counted strips, 1958. Note our car.

I didn't have many real paying jobs in high school. I worked at the mill on Saturday mornings helping Dad figure out how much of the wood in the logs the mill had purchased actually went into veneer and how much was waste that went into the boiler. I remember that some weeks he wasn't pleased with what my calculations showed.

I had to keep track by species of wood. The mill had paid more for some species than others, and Dad was sometimes surprised if he got more veneer out of the expensive logs than usual.

Dad's good friend Charley Barrett was often at the mill on Saturday mornings in the winter because he had closed his fish store for the season. Charley often asked me questions about topics I had never thought about.

"Marilyn, what stocks do you think I should buy?"

"I have no idea," I said.

"Marilyn, what kind of car should Sue and I buy next?"

"I have no idea."

"Marilyn, what color should it be?"

"I like blue," I said.

And so it went. Charley was always trying to get me to stretch my mind.

My other regular paying job was church organist, where my income was less than my parents paid for my organ lessons.

For two summers, I worked at the front desk of the St. Regis Hotel during the afternoon. The hotel was across from Lake Switzerland and I usually rode my bike and parked it at the back of the hotel. There was no need to lock it. Bike theft was very uncommon in Fleischmanns.

Mrs. Schumer, the owner, was a very smart businesswoman and a wonderful lady. I loved working for her. She called a spade a spade and God help you if you got on her wrong side.

The job was easy because all of the guests were napping. I had almost no customers.

One of my responsibilities was to type up the dinner menu. Mrs. Schumer would tell me what the menu was going to be and I would type it up. Then she posted the menu outside the dining room for the guests to read as they went in. One day, much to Mrs.

Schumer's amusement, I typed that one of the dinner choices was "soul" (instead of sole). She laughed, said the guests would be amused, and didn't make me retype the menu.

Another of my assignments was to go through the hotel's bar slips and ascertain how many ounces of each kind of liquor had been sold the previous night. To do this, I had to learn what liquors were used in each type of drink. Mrs. Schumer gave me the recipes.

One day, Mrs. Schumer said, "He's cheating me again. He does it every year. I'm calling him up here."

The next thing I knew, the bartender was in the office and Mrs. Schumer was saying, "You're doing it to me again. Every year we go through this. You're stealing from me." She then listed how many shots of liquor were in each bottle, how many bottles the slips indicated he had used, how many drinks had been paid for, and how many more bottles of liquor had been used according to her inventory and purchase records.

The bartender just stood there hanging his head. She then said, "I understand that you give one or two shots out of a bottle for a setup, and sometimes you spill some or mix the wrong kind of drink, but there is a lot more than that missing. So, stop it! I'll give you one more chance, but if you keep stealing from me, I'll fire you." He was still there when the season ended.

Another job I had was being a chambermaid for our neighbor Ruth Carey. When the Park Terrace Hotel, which was across the street and at the end of the ballpark, was full, it would send its overflow guests to Ruth's house. She had four bedrooms upstairs and the guests all shared a bathroom in the middle of the second floor. The bathroom had a bathtub, but no shower. I was always glad that when we went on vacation we didn't stay at a place where we had to share a bathroom with strangers.

As we were making beds and dusting, Ruth would tell me that she took in roomers during the summer to help her pay her real estate taxes. I barely knew what she was talking about. I didn't realize that if you owned a home, you had to pay the government money. My mother explained to me that people who own real estate have to pay school taxes and other taxes to maintain the roads and things. It made no sense to me that Ruth and Grandma Mayes had to pay school taxes even though they had no children in school.

Ruth was the secretary and bookkeeper for a garage in Margaretville. To my parents' disgust, her salary wasn't enough for her to pay all of her bills.

"Not only does she have to take in roomers in addition to working at the garage to pay her bills, she feels she has to be village treasurer as well. The garage should pay her a living wage. She is a very loyal employee," Dad commented to Mother on numerous occasions.

Since Ruth had a paralyzed leg from polio, she always said she was lucky to get any job at all. My parents always said she was very capable and that she shouldn't let her handicap stand in the way of earning a decent wage.

More than once, Ruth had guests who didn't pull their shades when they undressed at night. During the summer, Dean occupied Grandma Cowan's bedroom and, because of his great powers of observation, he always knew when one of these guests was at Ruth's. His bedroom had the best view of Ruth's house, so that is where we went for the peep show. Once we all had secured an excellent view of the upstairs windows of Ruth's house, we turned out all of the lights in Dean's room and waited. Since the guests were old, they tended to go to bed early. We seldom had to wait long before the show began. But, for better or worse, all we ever saw were ladies who were eighty if they were a day. As a result, we didn't watch long. There was always something better on TV, even if we got only one channel.

Chapter 21

Molly Goldberg's Funeral

Gertrude Berg's tombstone, 2013

One of most interesting things I witnessed in Fleischmanns in the 1960s was Molly Goldberg's funeral. I was seventeen, and it took place on Wagner Avenue, in the road, right in front of the synagogue in September 1966. We had heard on the radio that Gertrude Berg, known nationally as Molly Goldberg, had died. Dean had heard in his wanderings uptown (a.k.a. Main Street) that Molly's funeral was going to be in Fleischmanns and she would be buried in the Jewish cemetery in Clovesville, a suburb (if you will) of Fleischmanns. (Everyone I know calls this settlement "Clovesville," but, interestingly, the sign on the side of the road calls the settlement "Covesville.")

Molly Goldberg was a local celebrity. Even though, to the best of my knowledge, she didn't visit Fleischmanns when I was a child, I was familiar with her name because Grandma Mayes sometimes talked about her. In the 1930s and 1940s, Grandma Mayes (and the rest of America) had listened to her radio shows *The Rise of the Goldbergs* and *The Goldbergs*.

Molly's father had owned a boarding house in Fleischmanns when Molly was a teenager, and Grandma Mayes remembered seeing him around town. In the early 1950s, Molly had a television show, but I don't remember ever seeing it.

In anticipation of her funeral, we kept going out the front door, down the porch steps, and just a few feet up our front sidewalk so we could see if there was any activity at the synagogue. Soon there was a hearse and quite a few impressive black limousines parked in front of the synagogue. We kids walked up the street to listen and watch the goings-on. The back doors of the hearse were open and about thirty people were standing in the road near the hearse. We listened to what people were saying, but we couldn't understand most of it because it was in Hebrew.

The whole thing was over in no time. The next thing we knew, they closed up the back doors of the hearse and we heard someone say, "Let's drive around the block three times." And that is exactly what they did. They went up Wagner Avenue to Bridge Street, turned left onto Bridge Street, then left onto the part of Main Street that follows the stream, left onto Depot Street, past the Cat's Meow bar and restaurant, and finally left to come up Wagner Avenue, passing our house, the ballpark, and the synagogue. On the final trip, they didn't turn left on to Depot Street. Rather, they kept going straight to the cemetery, which was about half a mile away.

While this was going on, we kids ran home to get our bikes so we could be at the cemetery in time for the interment. We got there in time, but since we weren't properly attired, we thought it best if we hid behind a few sizable nearby gravestones.

More words were said, and then the strangest thing happened. I have checked this out with my brothers and we all agree this is what we saw. The casket had been partially lowered into the ground so that the top of it was slightly aboveground. People were looking at it and wiping their eyes. All of a sudden, we saw a young man throw a short knife into the lid of the casket. Thud. The point stuck. Some of the mourners shook their heads left and right, but no one said anything we could hear. They acted like this happens at every funeral. It was new to us, not having been to many funerals but having seen a lot of them on TV and in the movies.

The casket was then lowered to its final resting place and most of the mourners filed past it. Some of them put a shovelful of dirt on the casket. What a sound the dirt made as it hit the casket! After that, they all got back into their big black cars and left.

We got on our bikes and raced home to tell Mother what we had just witnessed. She said she hadn't been to any funerals where people threw a knife into the casket.

Chapter 22

Brian's Jeep

Brian's jeep, 1969

On the morning of July 24, 1968, Mother took Brian to the New York State Department of Motor Vehicles office in Delhi, New York, to get his learner's permit. This is all Brian wanted for his sixteenth birthday—aside from a car, which he knew was a long shot.

I was home that summer, having just completed my first year of college. Since I had my license, I frequently served as the adult driver who accompanied Brian while he honed his driving skills. He didn't need much practice because he had been driving our parents' car all around the mill yard for years. He was already an expert at parallel parking and three-point turns. He just needed some practice handling oncoming traffic. Needless to say, that didn't take long. In about three weeks, he had taken and passed his road test.

Then the serious pestering started. "Mom, when can I get a car?" he asked at least once a day.

"You know now that Fleischmanns High School has merged with Margaretville, I will have to take the late bus home because of basketball practice unless I get a car," he usually used as an argument. "Besides, I can do some errands for you and you wouldn't have to take me to work."

Both of our parents knew how important basketball was to Brian. As a sophomore, he was a starter on the last varsity basketball team Fleischmanns High School had. And, what a team it was. That year, the team won the league championship. Fleischmanns High School hadn't been league champions since 1956. The school was the smallest school in the league. There were only ten boys on the team and the team broke the school record for most points scored in a game when it scored 113 points.

Mother's usual answer to Brian's request for a car was, "I need to talk to your father. You know, it's expensive to own two cars."

At the time, Brian worked at Todd's garage, where he pumped gas. Self-service gas stations hadn't yet been invented. So Brian's job was to put gas in cars and, if the driver wanted, to check the oil, the antifreeze, and the windshield washer fluid levels. Drivers often tipped him anywhere from twenty-five cents to one dollar. On a very good day, he earned as much as five dollars in tips.

Todd's garage was also a Ford dealership. As such, it had quite a few used cars and trucks for sale.

For months, Brian had been coming home with reports of one used vehicle or another that he thought would be just perfect for our parents to buy for him.

Then, one day in late August, he came home with the news that Todd's had just taken a 1945 Willys army jeep in trade. He'd had a long discussion with Dan, the chief mechanic at the garage, and reported that Dan thought, with a little work, the jeep would run just fine. He thought Todd's would sell it for about five hundred dollars.

"Mom, can I take it for a test drive?" he asked.

"Okay, but I'm not promising that we'll buy it," Mother said.

The next Saturday afternoon, Brian and Mother went up to Todd's. Oscar Todd put dealer plates on the jeep and off Brian went to test it on the public roadways around town. While it had a few problems, like brakes that barely worked and virtually no second gear, Brian was confident that Dan could fix everything.

On Sunday, Brian, Dean, Brian's best friend Steve, and I went on a real test drive. We took dirt roads and wannabe roads such as former carriage roads, logging paths, and streambeds, both dry and not so dry. We went up and down very steep terrain testing both first gear and reverse. We didn't have a topo map and often didn't know exactly where we were. We usually had a general sense of which side of the mountain we were on or which valley we were in. When in doubt, we just headed downhill. Eventually we would come to a maintained dirt road, then we would come upon a hunting cabin or abandoned house with an outhouse and no electricity, and finally we would see utility poles with wires going in to a real house or modern cabin. Civilization at last.

We tested out what the vehicle could do in two-wheel drive with the hubs locked, (which we learned doesn't do anything); two-wheel drive with the hubs unlocked; high range four-wheel drive (with the hubs locked); and low-range four-wheel drive. We scraped the oil pan a few times and all had to get out (except for Brian, the driver) to lighten the load to prevent the oil pan from being torn off. Several times one or two of us got out to guide Brian as he turned the jeep around when we were in a particularly tight spot. By "tight spot" I mean places where turning around meant backing up onto a boulder and trying not to have the jeep slide off so that it would become hung up and stranded.

After a few hours of back-road and no-road traveling, Steve said to Brian as we got out yet again to lighten the load, "Brian, aren't you supposed to have nuts on all of the bolts that hold the wheel on to the axle?"

"Yes. Let me look," Brian said as he hopped out of the jeep. "We have a problem here. Do you guys realize we could shear the bolts off and lose a wheel?"

After observing that two, maybe three, bolts were missing, Brian went to the back of the jeep and got a lug wrench. As he was handing it to Steve, he said, "Steve, when I drive forward a few inches, use this lug wrench to pound the wheel back on to the axle."

"I'll try. I sure don't think they could ever get a tow truck in here to rescue this vehicle. And besides, I'm not looking forward to walking home from here," Steve said as he chuckled.

Brian stopped the jeep every few feet (we were on very rough terrain) to let Steve check the wheel and pound it back onto the bolts. When we finally got to paved roads, the wheel didn't need as much pounding and we arrived home, safe and sound.

On these test runs, we discovered that reverse had more power than first gear and that the jeep would pop out of second gear when the engine was under compression. That is, when we used the braking power of the engine because we had such poor brakes. Fortunately, the gearshift was a typical three-speed shift pattern and second gear was achieved by pushing the shifter toward the front of the jeep. So keeping the jeep in second was just a matter of keeping your hand pushed against the shifter to keep it from popping out of gear. What do you expect from a twenty-plus-year-old army surplus machine?

On Sunday evening, after taking the jeep back to Todd's, Brian reported to Mother and Dad that the jeep passed all of his tests. He was sure Dan could fix everything that was wrong so it would pass inspection.

The next morning, Oscar called Mother and asked her where the front dealer plate was. He explained that if someone put it on a vehicle, he was concerned his insurance would have to cover the vehicle if it were in an accident. He didn't want to take that risk. At lunch, Mother asked us if we had any idea where the plate could be. Dad grinned and said, "Tell Oscar not to worry. Where these kids went, no one will find it." It was one of the few times I saw our father so casual about something like this.

The following weekend, Mother and Brian went to Todd's and Mother bought the jeep. Yes, the jeep was titled in Mother's name. She never drove it, but admitted it was worth every penny she and Dad spent on it.

Brian drove the jeep everywhere. Naively, Mother always thought he was safe since the jeep's top speed was about fifty miles per hour. Both Brian and Mother were happy.

In December 1968, I was home from college for Christmas vacation. Aunt Gerry, Uncle Jim, and Danny, who was also in college, came up from Florida to visit family and friends.

One evening, the adults were in the living room visiting and we kids were trying to think of things to do. Brian said to Danny, "Want to go for a spin in my jeep?"

"Sure," Danny said.

"Let's go up to Halcott and take the road over to Red Kill," I said.

We had had quite a bit of snow recently, but that day had been very sunny with temperatures in the mid-thirties. Now it was a beautiful, clear, and calm winter evening with the stars out and the temperature in the mid-twenties. The snowbanks were three to four feet high.

Brian drove, Danny sat in the front passenger's seat, I sat behind Brian, and Dean sat behind Danny. The roads were clear in the village, but as we got to Halcott, the road was clear only in the tracks where cars and trucks had gone. When Brian turned off onto the road to Red Kill, it was obvious that few people traveled this road. It had been plowed, but it was covered with snow and had icy spots because of the warmth and sun earlier in the day. At this point, Brian and Danny got out and locked the hubs so we could use four-wheel drive. They piled back in and off we went. Brian was showing Danny how fast the jeep could go in four-wheel drive when we suddenly came upon a sharp curve to the left that Brian had forgotten about. Or, at least, it came up sooner than he anticipated.

He cranked the steering wheel hard to the left and the jeep's tires on the left side came up off of the road. The next thing we knew, the jeep tipped about forty-five degrees to the right and came to rest on the passenger side. The snowbank was holding it up. In an attempt to right the jeep, we all moved to the left in our seats, gripping whatever was nearby. Of course, the jeep didn't have seat belts. It was made before they were invented. With the shift in weight, the jeep righted itself as fast as it went onto its side. The left tires hit the road with a thud and we all sat upright. There was total silence.

"Well, that was exciting. Do you do that often?" Danny asked a few seconds later.

"Boy, that was close," Brian said.

Then we all started to laugh.

The jeep didn't get any more dents or scratches because of this adventure and, miraculously, the canvas top and sides didn't rip.

When we got home, Aunt Gerry said, "How was your trip?"

"Great. Just great," Danny said. Then the four of us gave a nervous laugh.

"Let's go get some soda," Brian suggested, whereupon the four of us departed for the safety of the kitchen.

The next day at breakfast, Mother said to us, "How did Danny like the jeep ride?"

Of course, we had to tell her what happened. This story was too good to keep to ourselves.

"I knew something had happened by the way you kids acted when you got back. Good thing no one was hurt," Mother said.

The following spring, I was home from college on spring break and Brian asked me if I wanted to drive the jeep while he sat in the front passenger's seat with his .22–250 rifle and shot woodchucks. Of course I said yes. This sounded like an interesting way to while away an hour or two. So off we went to Halcott, where there were a lot of hayfields with woodchucks.

Brian explained that he was doing the farmers a favor. He told me farmers don't like woodchucks in their fields because of all of the tunnels and holes they make. However, after he shot three or four woodchucks, I must confess, when he spotted the next few, I accelerated rather than slowed down, thus saving the lives of a few of them. After a few such accelerations, he threatened to fire me as his driver.

On one of these trips, it started to rain so I turned on the windshield wiper. There was only one big wiper that wiped the driver's side and a small portion of the passenger's side. If you had a passenger, the passenger moved a very small wiper to clear the rest of the window on the passenger's side by grabbing a small handle on the inside of the windshield and moving the handle left and right to clean that side of the windshield. Both wipers were attached to the top of the windshield.

To be charitable, I'll characterize the wiper on the driver's side as an early and unreliable version of today's intermittent wipers. When you stepped on the accelerator, the wiper slowed down. If you put the accelerator to the floor because you were on a steep hill, the wiper stopped completely. So if it was raining cats and dogs and you wanted to go up a steep hill, you had a choice: either barely move and risk being rear-ended, but be able to see where you wanted to go; or go up the hill at a respectable speed and have to guess where the road was. I usually fluctuated between the two, which made for a very uncomfortable ride.

Whenever I complained about the horrid wiper, Brian patiently explained that a vacuum that was created in the engine compartment controlled the driver's side wiper. He would then point to a small box inside the jeep directly behind the wiper on the driver's side. A rubber tube went from the box, around the windshield, and disappeared into the engine compartment. The vacuum made its way to the box via the rubber tube.

Many of our jeep rides were in the summer, right after supper. One evening, Brian said, "Mom, want to go for a ride in my jeep?"

"I guess so. I have nothing going on tonight," she said.

So, Brian and Mother got in the front seats and Dean and I got in the back seat. This was one of the few times Mother rode in the jeep and I wasn't about to miss seeing her reaction. I figured Brian had something up his sleeve.

We went up to Halcott, turned around, and, on our way back to Fleischmanns, we took the road that goes over to Red Kill. We came upon a bump in the road and instead of slowing down, Brian accelerated. The tires didn't come off of the road, but the jeep was at the top of its suspension.

"Brian, slow down!" Mother shouted.

"Oh Mom, that's nothing. We didn't even get airborne," Brian said.

Then we three kids laughed and Mother was trying to figure out whether to laugh or be mad.

We were still going at a pretty good clip when, the next thing I knew, the road seemed to disappear. We were going up a hill and all you could see was the horizon. I had no idea if the road turned left or right or just went on straight.

"Brian, slow down!" Mother shouted again.

"Mom, I've done this hundreds of times. Relax. I know what I'm doing." And a few seconds later, he laughed and said, "Wasn't that fun?"

As we three kids all laughed, even Mother had to admit she was having fun.

Brian was having so much fun riding around in his ancient jeep; it occurred to me that he needed a costume to go with it. So one day when I was in Kingston to buy shoes, I bought fake leather fabric and, after much searching in the pattern books, found a pattern to make Brian a hat like the airplane pilots wore in World War I, chin strap and all. I wasn't the world's best seamstress, but the hat did fit. He looked a little like the Red Baron as he drove around town.

During the following winter, Brian used the snow-covered roads to perfect handling the jeep when it was in a skid. He went to vacant, snow-covered parking lots to develop a feel for how fast he could go and still maintain control of a skid. He learned how to slide the jeep where he wanted it to go by driving at just the right speed, cranking the steering wheel, and applying the brakes at just the right time.

As a result, in the winter, Brian almost never drove into the driveway to our house. He would put the jeep into a skid and slide into the driveway, narrowly missing both the telephone pole that was about ten feet from the entrance to the driveway and the famous pine tree that was about twenty feet down the driveway and six feet into the yard.

Upon watching Brian come into the driveway, Mother frequently said to Dad, "One of these days he's going to misjudge."

He never did.

Since I was in college during most of Brian's adventures with his jeep, I missed some important events. I'll never forget the day I came home from college on spring break and there was a black and yellow tiger-striped jeep sitting in the driveway. I couldn't believe my eyes. Who did this belong to? As I got out of the car, Brian came out of the house and said, "Like my jeep? Steve and I painted it a few weeks ago."

"Wow, sure is unique," I said. "But don't think you can hide very well if the police are ever looking for you."

"Oh, don't worry about that," Brian said as he laughed.

Brian drove the jeep for about three years before it died of natural causes. It had provided him with so much entertainment and our parents thought jeeps were so much safer than a car that they bought Dean one when he turned sixteen.

Chapter 23

How Did This All End?

Brian, Dean, and me, 2013

So, how did we three turn out?

During Christmas vacation of my senior year of college, Mother said to me, "So, what do you plan to do next year?"

Truthfully, I was so absorbed in studying that I hadn't given the matter any thought, and I said so. Then Mother said, "Well, you like to argue. Daddy and I wonder if you'd like to become an attorney?"

"Never thought of that. There certainly is some truth to the fact that I like to argue."

The last major argument I had with my mother was the spring of my senior year in college. It was over my wedding.

I was married in August 1971. Stan and I wanted a very small, hippie type of wedding, and we had been thinking of having it in the dining room of my parents' house. But my mother wanted to invite a lot of the people to the wedding.

"I owe all of these people an invitation," Mother said, pointing to a long list of names. "After all, Daddy and I were invited to their daughter's wedding, this couple's thirtieth wedding anniversary party, and she just gave her daughter a very nice baby shower that I went to."

"Well, have your own party," I replied. "You don't have to use my wedding as an excuse to repay your social debts." And so it went for weeks.

"You know that Aunt Inez and Aunt Glad don't care about a party. They really want to see you get married," Mother often used as an argument. They were Grandma Mayes's sisters and I loved both of them dearly.

"You know I want to get married in this house, not in the church. I don't want all of those people on Main Street gawking at Stan and me as we come out of the church. My wedding is none of their business," I replied.

Finally we came to the grand compromise: Stan and I would get married in the dining room. Stan's family, our attendants, our siblings, Grandma Mayes, my aunts, uncles, and great-aunts would be invited to the wedding. (Grandma Cowan and my great-uncles were already dead.) Then Mother could invite whomever she wanted to the reception.

I wanted to be married facing the big window that looked out toward Ruth Carey's house. It was usually a sunny spot, especially in August. A day after I announced this, Mother quietly explained to me that

Dad didn't want me to be married there. This was the spot Dad's father had lain in his casket and where the family had greeted people during calling hours.

Wow, that was the first I had heard this.

Mother explained that it was common years ago to have the deceased person brought home before the funeral. She then went on to say that this was what she and Dad wanted for themselves, in that very spot.

Mother then suggested I get married facing the wall where the buffet sat, with Stan's and my backs to the front door. I readily agreed. Then, pointing first in one direction of the dining room and then another, I said, "I get it. That window is for funerals and that wall is for weddings."

Mother laughed and said, "Something like that."

The only problem with the wall where the buffet sat was that there was a very big water stain on the wallpaper, caused by a leak in the roof. My parents had been fighting the roof leaks caused by snow and ice dams for years. It always seemed that just as they thought they had fixed the problem and had rooms repapered, a leak would appear in a new spot. Since this was a persistent problem, whenever Mother had a room papered, she ordered several extra rolls of paper so she could have sections of a room repapered.

Realizing that Dean had a lot of experience with writing on wallpaper, Mother had Dean scribble on the white-on-white wallpaper with white chalk in an attempt to cover up the stain. It didn't work. Fortunately, there was extra wallpaper in the attic so she had the paperhanger come and properly fix the area.

The wedding and reception went off as planned except for one detail. Dean, who was fifteen at the time, sat at the bar of the restaurant where my reception was held. His goal was to drink twelve whiskey sours. Well, halfway through number eleven, he threw up all over the bar.

I didn't know a thing about this until Stan and I went back to the house to change our clothes for our honeymoon. When we drove into the driveway, we noticed Dean sprawled out on the grass with my cousin Ruth sitting beside him. He was the same color as the grass and very under the weather.

"What's wrong with him?" I asked Ruth.

"Just a little too much to drink is all. Ain't nothin' a little time won't cure. Just go on and enjoy yourselves," Ruth assured us.

Dean did survive but even forty-one years later isn't able to tolerate even the smell of a whiskey sour.

A few years later, Grandma Mayes died. When Stan and I went home for the funeral, we walked through the dining room to take our suitcases upstairs. There, beside the large dining room window, was Gram's casket with the lid down. No one had warned me she would be there. I guess Mother just expected me to remember from the days of our discussions about where to have my wedding.

Aunt Gerry, Uncle Jim, and Danny had arrived from Florida and were also staying at the house. Aunt Gerry and Uncle Jim were sleeping in Dean's room. So where did Dean sleep? Right on the dining room floor beside the casket.

My parents didn't get their wish of having their caskets in the dining room. But it wasn't due to an argument with me or anyone else. They had sold the house and moved to live near us kids in the Albany, New York, region.

As Mother and Dad insightfully suggested, I did become an attorney. I was a tax attorney with New York State. I loved my job, most of the time. I live with my husband of forty-one years and our cat whose name is Al E. Cat.

Brian became a Ph.D. toxicologist and works in the private sector. He and his wife own and operate a Christmas tree farm. In his spare time, Brian makes wonderful furniture. Among the things he has made are an ash dining room table and six ash bent-wood chairs. He can fix nearly anything. He is especially fond of internal combustion engines. So he clearly inherited our great- and great-great-grandfathers' carpentry genes and our father's entrepreneurial genes.

Brian is a natural athlete, and whenever I challenge him to a game of anything that involves hand–eye coordination, such as croquet at a family reunion, he always wins.

Dean, always marching to the beat of his own drum, went to seven colleges before getting his B.A. in economics. Our parents always had faith that one day he would realize the benefits of an education, and they were right. As the chief information officer of a school district with nearly ten thousand students, one of the largest school districts in New York State, he oversaw a yearly budget of $4.5 million. He and his wife now own and operate a handmade, goat-milk soap business. They have customers in all fifty states and U.S. territories and thirty-eight countries. So he too has our father's entrepreneurial spirit. He can also fix nearly anything.

My brothers and I live within an hour of each other, near Albany. While we don't get together that often, when we do certain patterns emerge.

We are all very independent and try to think things through on our own. We tend not to accept something as true just because it was printed in some newspaper or journal, especially if it is counterintuitive. This must stem from all of those experiments we did in the laundry room on Sunday afternoons.

We all like to laugh and can be seriously entertained by the smallest incident. I'm sure this flows from all those times we patiently waited for a customer to pick up the wallet tied to a string that we hung from the tree house.

We always discuss which way food should be passed when we sit down to dinner. It never matters which way, we just want it all to go the same way.

At Christmastime, we relive the Christmas Eve service we went to with Mother at the Halcott Methodist Church two or three years after I was married.

Stan and I were at my parents' on Christmas Eve day in the mid-1970s. In the late afternoon, we all ate appetizers and everyone (except Mother) had several drinks. In those years, the legal age for consuming alcohol was eighteen. Mother never liked the taste of alcoholic beverages, so she seldom had more than one very weak brandy alexander.

At dinner, we decided it would be nice to go to an early candlelight service. It had snowed that day, the sky was clear, and there was a nearly full moon. It was a beautiful winter evening. Since none of us were in any of the activities at the Fleischmanns church, we had a choice of where to go.

Mother said, "You know, they're having an early candlelight service up at the Halcott church, if you kids want to go to that. I'm sure it will be a pretty drive."

"Oh, let's go. That's such a pretty little church and I haven't been there or to the head of Halcott in a very long time," I said.

We ate dinner quickly and Dad stayed behind to put the dishes in the dishwasher. He said he'd rather rest than go.

We brushed the snow off of two cars, piled in, and off we went. It was a beautiful drive up the snow-covered mountain road. It took about thirty minutes to get to the church.

We all noisily traipsed into the very small church, stomping the snow off of our boots as we went.

"Boy, we barely got here in time," Mother said as we found two pews near the back that could accommodate us. There were forty to fifty people in the church; it was nearly full.

"Do you have enough room?" I said to Mother as Stan tried to move over to make more room.

"Yes, I'm fine. Shh, they are about to start," Mother said, placing her right index finger across her lips, turning to look at me, and then turning around to look at Brian and Dean.

I looked through the church bulletin. *Good, it's going to be just some readings from the Bible about the birth of Jesus, interspersed with a few hymns and a prayer or two. This shouldn't take too long,* I thought.

We were halfway through the service and about to sing the third hymn, "O Little Town of Bethlehem." Not my favorite hymn because it is in a minor key. *Christmas is supposed to be a joyful occasion, so why is this a popular hymn?* I wondered.

I sure hope the pianist doesn't let the congregation slow this hymn down too much. Mrs. Truran (my organ teacher) was always warning me about how this could happen if the organist let it.

I was lost in thought and caught only a few words of what the minister was saying. He said something about a typo in the bulletin and we were to sing only two verses, or maybe he said three.

Why can't the pianist speed up this hymn? At this speed, it's worse than ever. It's getting slower and slower. At least when I play, we get through it quickly. Mrs. Truran was right about what sometimes happens, I thought.

After the first verse, the pianist paused before starting the second verse. *Big mistake,* I thought. *This gives the slowest people time to finish. You should just start the next verse quickly, they'll get the idea,* I thought.

After the second verse, the same thing happened. Hoping to speed things up, I belted out in my off-key singing voice, "For Christ is . . ." I stopped because, not only did the pianist not join me, no one else did either.

Oh dear. Must be he said we are singing only two verses, I thought. *How embarrassing.*

I looked at Stan. He was trying to contain his laughter.

"A little too much celebration before dinner?" Dean leaned forward and asked me in too loud a voice for comfort. At least twenty people turned around and looked at me. A few of them smiled but others gave a look that indicated we all should have stayed at home, given our condition.

"Sure hope we don't burn the place down when we light the candles," Brian said in a loud stage whisper. Then we all started to laugh uncontrollably.

By this time in the service, I was a little less inebriated. *What a beautiful church,* I thought. *I sure am glad we made the effort to come, even if no one else in this church is.*

When we got home, Mother couldn't wait to tell Dad. He just smiled and said, "Guess they'll be talking about that for a while."

Another tradition we have continued at family get-togethers is Bonanza Rummy. After a family dinner, we get out the poker chips, a deck of cards, and the Bonanza Rummy game. The generation below us participates in borrowing and lending chips and we still discuss if we should charge interest. We never do. It was only recently one of the younger generation, now in his mid-twenties, confessed that he was in high school when he realized that at the end of the Bonanza Rummy game all of the chips were put back in their boxes and no money ever changed hands.

We still have family reunions with my mother's side of the family. My brothers, my cousins, many of their children, and a few of their grandchildren attend. Our relatives are now spread all over the United States. The reunions are every two years, and recent ones have been held in Margaretville, New York; Breckenridge, Colorado; and Clayton, North Carolina. The next one is at Dean's, near Albany.

For the last twenty years, we have had a square dance band at our reunions. We always have lots of food and often no alcohol because this isn't a drinking crowd. People come from Alabama, California, Connecticut, Colorado, Ohio, North Carolina, South Carolina, and New York.

So, while none of us have the last name of Cowan or Koutz any more, the family tradition of gathering every few years continues for yet another generation even though we now live all over the country.

Murray's Knot

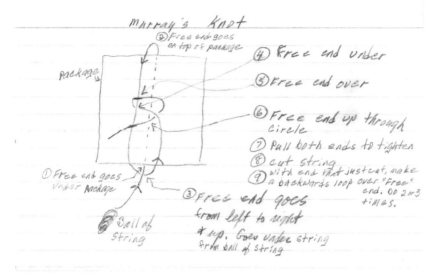

Diagram of the knot my father used to tie bundles of
veneer (and anything else that needed tying)

Family Recipes for Items Mentioned in the Book

I am providing these recipes because I think they may be of historical interest. The hot-water-bath canning method is *not* recommended today, and modern refrigeration methods should be used to make corned beef.

Banana Cake
Grandma (Nellie) Mayes's recipe

½ cup butter
1¼ cups sugar
2 eggs, well beaten
1¾ cups cake flour or 2 cups regular flour
½ teaspoon salt
½ teaspoon baking powder
¾ teaspoon baking soda
½ cup sour milk (she made sour milk by adding a little vinegar to regular milk)
½ cup mashed bananas
1 teaspoon vanilla

Cream the butter, sugar, and eggs. Sift the flour, measure and sift again with baking soda, baking powder, and salt. Add the milk and flour mixture alternately, then the bananas and vanilla.

Bake at 375°F—no time given. Grandma Mayes used two 8" or 9" diameter cake pans that were greased and coated with flour.

Grandma Mayes always baked a small amount of the cake before baking the whole thing to see if the batter needed more flour or milk.

Bread-and-Butter Pickles
Mother got this recipe from
Dick Pultz's mother, Lena Pultz.
I still make these.

4 quarts cucumbers, sliced
4 onions, sliced
2 sweet red peppers, sliced
1 green pepper, sliced
1 teaspoon turmeric
1 teaspoon ground mustard
4 teaspoons salt
2 teaspoons whole mustard seeds
3 cups sugar
3 cups vinegar

Bring spices, vinegar, and sugar to a boil. Add the cucumbers, onions, and peppers. Heat thoroughly and until vegetables are a little soft. Put the vegetables in sterilized canning jars.

Reheat the syrup and boil down some to reduce the volume. Pour over the vegetables and seal the jars.

Process the jars using the hot-water-bath canning method for 5 minutes.

Canned Beef
Mother probably got this recipe
from her mother.

10 pounds of beef (will yield about 9 pints)
Salt and pepper

Cut beef into 1" to 2" cubes. Moderately pepper the beef and pack into sterilized pint or quart canning jars. If using a pint jar, add ½ teaspoon of salt. If using a quart jar, add 1 teaspoon of salt.

Add water to fill the jar to within ½" of the top. Seal the jars and process using the hot-water-bath canning method for 3 hours.

Grape Juice
Mother

2 cups grapes, washed and left whole
½ cup sugar

Pack into sterilized quart canning jar. Fill with boiling water, seal, and turn upside down until cool.

Corned Beef
Based on recipes of Aunt Anna Morse and
Grandma (Anna) Cowan.

100 pounds of beef
5 pounds salt
1 quart molasses
2 ounces saltpeter

1 tablespoon cayenne pepper

Or

25 pounds of beef
1¼ pounds salt
1 cup molasses
½ ounce saltpeter
¼ teaspoon cayenne pepper

Add the last four ingredients to some water to make brine. Bring the brine to a boil. Put the beef in a stone crock and pour the brine over it (either hot or it can be cool). Add enough water to the brine to cover the beef. Be sure the brine fully covers the beef. Be sure to put a pie plate or dinner plate on the floating beef and add some weight to the plate so the brine will cover the beef.

Store in a very cool place or in the refrigerator. Will have corned beef in about 6 weeks. If the brine becomes cloudy or moldy, drain, strain, reheat to boiling, cool, and pour over the meat.

Ice Cream
Mother based this on
several of her cookbooks.

2 quarts milk
½ to ¾ cups flour
3 cups sugar
4 eggs, separated (beat the egg whites until they form peaks)
salt

vanilla
¾ pint to 1 quart heavy cream

Heat the milk in a double boiler. Stir in flour and sugar and heat until thickens. Add egg yolks and salt. Remove from heat and add beaten egg whites, cream, and vanilla. Put in an ice cream maker.

If you want to make chocolate ice cream, use 4 cups of sugar, ½ cup flour, and 6 ounces (squares) of chocolate. Add the chocolate at the end and be sure it all melts before putting the mixture in the ice cream maker.

Mustard Pickles
I think Mother based this
on Lena Pultz's recipe.

2 quarts small cucumbers, sliced
1 quart small onions, peeled
1 quart string beans, cut in half
2 quarts green tomatoes, cut in large pieces
1 quart carrots, cut in large pieces
2 quarts lima beans
2 heads cauliflower, cut in large pieces
6 green peppers

3 quarts vinegar
2 tablespoons ground mustard
¼ ounce turmeric
5 cups sugar
2 cups flour

Mix the vegetables with some salt and let them sit overnight. Then cook each vegetable separately in salted water until barely done.

Mix the flour in a little water and then add it to the vinegar, sugar, and spices.

Stir the vegetables into the vinegar mixture and then put everything into sterilized canning jars.

There are no notes as to whether the jars are then processed using the hot-water-bath canning method. I do remember that the jars had paraffin on top, so perhaps they were not processed.

Popcorn Balls
Aunt Anna Morse gave me this recipe
over the phone in 1964.

½ cup sugar
2/3 cup molasses
2 teaspoon butter
2 teaspoon vinegar
large batch popcorn

Boil the first four ingredients until the mixture reaches the soft-ball stage. That is, until a soft ball forms when you drop a little in a glass of cold water.

Let mixture cool a little and then pour over popcorn. Make into balls. Yummmmm!